FILUI

A Pl

Eduardo de ⅃⅃⅃

English version by
Keith Waterhouse
&
Willis Hall

SAMUEL FRENCH

LONDON
NEW YORK TORONTO SYDNEY HOLLYWOOD

FILUMENA

First presented by Danny O'Donovan, Alan Cluer and Helen Montagu at the Lyric Theatre, London, on the 2nd November 1977, with the following cast of characters:

Filumena Marturano	Joan Plowright
Domenico Soriano	Colin Blakely
Alfredo Amoroso	Larry Noble
Rosalia Solimene	Patricia Hayes
Diana	Sharon Mughan
Lucia	Jane Gurnett
Umberto	Christopher Guard
Riccardo	Trevor Eve
Michele	Larry Lamb
Nocella	David Graham
Teresina	Linda Polan
Waiters	Trevor Griffiths
	Edward Duke

The play directed by Franco Zeffirelli
Setting by Raimonda Gaetani

The action takes place in Domenico Soriano's house
ACT I   Late evening in Spring
ACT II   The following day
ACT III Ten months later

Time—1946

ACT I*

A large dining-room in the house of Domenico Soriano. The last light of day is just leaving the terrace on a late Spring evening

The room is expensively furnished, if not in the best of taste. There are paintings and pieces which have been inherited by Domenico from his parents and which clash with the modern furnishings. To one side in the back wall glass doors open on to a glassed-in passage way leading to the terrace and also to the kitchen. On the other side of the back wall is an opening to a small hallway: an outer door leads from this to the front door, off; and a passage to other parts of the house. There are two other doors, one to the bedroom, the other to Domenico's study. On an ornate sideboard are displayed the cups and other trophies which have been won by his racehorses. The large dining-table has been laid, elegantly, for a meal for two. There is a bowl of red roses in the middle of the table

Standing in the doorway of the bedroom, her arms folded defiantly across her bosom, is Filumena Marturano. She is wearing a long nightdress. Her hair is untidy and she is wearing bedroom slippers. Her face is that of a woman who has known a hard life. Filumena is not coarse—but she is from a working-class background and is not ashamed of the fact. She is frank, demonstrative and a decisive woman. She is forty-eight, but does not look it. Though her hair may be turning silver at the temples, her eyes have an almost youthful brightness—they are gleaming now at the prospect of the argument to come and of which she is not afraid. In the opposite corner, downstage, stands her adversary, Domenico Soriano, a well-built man of about fifty who has enjoyed life to the full. He is wearing trousers and a pyjama jacket. On the other side of the room, by the terrace, stands Rosalia Solimene, seventy-five years old, wearing a black dress. She has known Filumena since she was a little girl. In the fourth corner of the room stands Alfredo Amoroso, about sixty years of age, who has been Domenico's faithful servant and good friend for many years

---

*N.B. Paragraph 3 on page ii of this Acting Edition regarding photocopying and video-recording should be carefully read.

When the CURTAIN *rises, we discover these four confronting one another from the four corners of the room as if they were engaged in playing some sort of game—but we soon discover that this is no game*

Domenico (*hitting himself hard across the face, again and again*) Crazy! Crazy! Crazy! Crazy! A hundred times. A thousand times. Crazy.

Alfredo (*genuinely concerned*) Domenico! Don't, you will hurt yourself!

Rosalia goes to the bedroom and fetches a shawl which she puts round Filumena's shoulders

Domenico (*ignoring him*) I am worthless. I should go now to the nearest mirror and spit in my own face. (*To Filumena*) All that I was, I have given to you. I have given you myself for twenty-five years—my brain, my body, my youth. What more do you want? What more is there of Domenico Soriano that you have not already had? You have taken my sanity—I am insane! Do you want the skin too? Do you want what is left of the flesh? Would you like my dry bones? (*To all three of them*) You've all had your own way. I thought I was Jesus Christ on earth and behind my back you crucified me! (*Turning to each one in turn*) You—you—you in this street, in this neighbourhood, in Naples—on this earth you have destroyed me! (*Back to Filumena*) When I think of it I can't think straight. If I tried to sit down now and put my mind to what you've done I would have to get up and walk round the room! I should have known. It's in your nature. A woman like you, how else should I expect you to behave? Even after twenty-five years of living with me—of course, you'll go back to your old ways. But don't think you've won. I'll see you in your grave first, woman. You, and all those who have helped you. The doctor. The priest. (*To Rosalia and Alfredo*) And you two jackals—you've had your last meal off my carcass. I'll see the pair of you in hell too, I'll put a bullet into each of you. Where's my revolver?

Alfredo At the gunsmith's.

Domenico What's it doing at the gunsmith's?

Alfredo You told me to take it—the barrel is rusty.

Domenico (*back to Filumena*) We are finished, you and I. Completely. You will leave this house—this is my house and you will get out of it. And if you don't walk out, by God, I tell you they will carry you out, woman. Dead. No-one defies Domenico Soriano. No-one. Try to fight me and I will smash you to pulp. I will see you all in jail. This house belongs to me. All that I own belongs to me. I am going to keep it, Filumena. You will dance to my tune. When I tell them who you were—what you were—the whore-house I found you in—do you think they'll listen then to you? You thought you'd destroyed me—but watch. Watch me, Filumena. I am going to destroy you. Prostitute!

Filumena Is that the end? Have you finished? Can I speak now?

Domenico Shut up! Don't speak. I don't want to hear your voice. I don't want to have to look into your face!

Filumena Don't worry. (*Pointing to her stomach*) When I have told you what is in here, you will never hear my voice again. And you won't have to look in my face.

Domenico (*with contempt*) Whore! You were a whore when I met you and, in your heart, you are still a whore!

Filumena Do we have to go into all that all over again? Everybody knows what I was. It isn't any secret. What I was, and where I lived—yes, and who came to visit me, too ! How many times were you there, Domenico, knocking on the door? You got the same service as all the rest. What have you got to complain about now? I know what I was. That's for me to cry over. I don't need you to remind me, and I know what I am now. I'm your wife. This is my house too. Fetch the police; if you like—I am not moving from my house.

Domenico I thought I was crazy—she is crazy. Wife? You whore! Who could marry a whore like you!

Filumena You! You! Man and wife! Me and you!

Domenico You *are* insane. You don't think you'll get away with that? (*He gestures at Alfredo and Rosalia*) I have witnesses, woman.

Rosalia Don't drag me into it. She was too ill to speak. She was in agony, that's all I know. She never said one word to me.

Domenico (*to Alfredo*) How about you? Didn't you know that with her dying breath she was living a lie?

Alfredo How could I? She hates me! She wouldn't tell me.

Rosalia (*to Domenico*) What about the priest? Who was the first to say that she was dying? Who sent for the priest?

Domenico Of course I sent for a priest. She was dying. She wanted a priest. I did what she told me.

Filumena You couldn't wait for the priest to get here. All you wanted was to see me out of this world.

Domenico If only you were out of it now! If only you'd been telling the truth. That priest believed her. I believed you. And I believed him too, when he said, "This poor woman is dying—marry her—it is her last wish on earth". Out of the goodness of my heart I agreed.

Filumena You agreed, because you have not got a heart to beat in your body. "She is only clinging on to life until I marry her," you thought. "The quicker I marry her, the quicker she will be dead."

Domenico Bravo!

Filumena It was a shock for you, wasn't it, when the priest had gone and I jumped out of bed? "Congratulations, we are man and wife."

Rosalia (*before Domenico can get a word in*) It was a shock for me, too. I jumped out of my chair. I was the one who nearly died. And then I saw the funny side. (*She begins to laugh*) I thought I'd see a wedding and a funeral in one week. You were very good. The way you took the part, you should have been an actress.

Alfredo What about the agony! I could almost feel the pain myself.

Domenico Shut up both of you, or you really will feel the pain. We are not man and wife. We will never be man and wife. Cannot be! (*With a sudden thought*) What about the doctor? Did you manage to fool him too or did you bribe him? Can't we even trust the medical profession any longer? Or was he as big an idiot as me?

Alfredo I think he was as big an idiot as you . . .

Domenico Shut up! He'll suffer for this. I will make him suffer for it. He was in your clutches, wasn't he? You tell me the truth—you bought him.

Filumena (*disgustedly*) Bought. Bought, bought. You think you can buy anything and everything and anybody.

Domenico Yes! Often enough, I've bought and paid for you!

Filumena Because you are Don Domenico Soriano. So you can buy whatever it is you want. You can buy the best shirts, hand-made. The best suits, hand-tailored. The best racehorses with the finest pedigree and, to make them win, you can hire the best jockeys to ride them. I have been your workhorse for twenty-five years, Don Domenico Soriano—but now it's my turn in the saddle. I hold the reins in my hand and I'm going to make you gallop. And, believe me, you have some galloping to do! Twenty-five years I have been a servant to you—a slave almost. Of course that doctor believed I was in agony. After twenty-five years of you any woman would be in agony. (*To the other two*) You two are witnesses to my life here. When he went off and enjoyed himself—London—Paris—Rome—did I ever go with him? No, no, he'd take a racehorse, not me. I had to stay behind. Well of course. Why not? I couldn't be his wife. I was not good enough to be his wife, but I was good enough to be left here in charge of everything. The factory at Forcella; the one at Virgene. The shops at Tuledo and in Foria. Because he is so well-loved by his workers that if I were not there, they would steal every penny he possesses. (*Giving her impression of the wheedling Domenico*) "What a wonderful woman you are, Filumini ... How could I ever begin to manage without you?" Very well, it seems, in Paris and London and Rome—it is only here that he cannot be without me. To look after his house. To look after his businesses. I have even got down and washed his feet for him.

Domenico Not any longer.

Filumena Not any longer—when I was a girl and didn't know any better. Never—not once did you show any appreciation for what I was doing. Not one word, not one sign to show thanks for it. I have never had respect in this house. What have I been here, for twenty-five years? Never anything except a maid, a servant, a slave.

Domenico What about me? Never have you shown me any appreciation of what I have done for you—not a hint of understanding of the difficult situation I have found myself in, living with a woman of your reputation. No. Always scowling —a cold-blooded housekeeper walking from one room to the next with a face as long as a wet week. You have never brought anything out into the open. It's always been inside you, brooding. You have worn a mask on your face. All the time we've lived together, I've never seen a tear in your eye. Do you realize that?

Filumena Did you expect me to cry because of you?

Domenico Because of anything. All women cry sometimes. Not you. There's something wrong with you. You are not human. It's normal to cry. It's as normal for a woman to cry as it is for her to eat or drink or sleep. Come to that, I've never even seen you sleep.

Filumena How could you see me sleeping? You're never here to see me sleep. You've forgotten the way home.

Domenico That is a lie!

Filumena Are the holidays a lie? Was Christmas a lie? Was Easter a lie? How many Christmases and how many Easters have I spent here on my own. No, you're right. I don't cry. Do you know what makes a woman cry? When she knows what happiness is, but it's beyond her reach. That's not me. Filumena Marturano has never known happiness. What she hasn't missed, she is unable to cry for. I would kill myself—cut out my heart myself—before I'd give you the pleasure of seeing me cry. You would think as he got older he might have changed. When he was younger you might have blamed it on the women who ran after him for his looks and money. But now, now. At his age. Look at him. He is fifty-two years old and he still comes back here, when he feels like it, with his handkerchiefs covered in lipstick. He throws them down for me to wash and I pick them up and I feel sick with disgust! (*To Rosalia*) Where are they now?

Rosalia Don't worry. If you ever need them they are very well hidden.

Filumena You would think that he would have thought of that himself. You might think that he might think it might be right for me not to see them. No. He throws them down. On the bedroom floor, the bathroom floor. "Why shouldn't she wash them", he thinks. "What is she? Nothing." I have had no rights in this house. But him—he has every right—even the right to carry on, in front of me, with that—that . . .

Domenico That what? That what?

Filumena That slut. That cow. Carrying on with that little bitch. Did you really think that I was blind? You've never been able to lie, that's your problem. You are fifty-two years old and you have no more brains than to run around with a twenty-two-year-old cow. And you have no shame that you can bring her inside this house. A nurse! Does she look like a nurse. No, she looks what she is—she looks like a cow. A nurse! Did you really think I would believe that? After I had taken one look at her? Yes—yes, you thought I would believe it, because you thought I was dying. (*Incredulously*) And less than one hour ago just before the priest came here, and asked you to marry me because I was standing on the threshold of death—and you agreed . . .

Domenico I agreed only because you lied . . .

Filumena You agreed, Domenico, you agreed to marry me. Less than one hour ago. You stood next to my bed and put your hands all over that cow, and touched her—and kissed her. (*Nauseated*) Madonna! You really make me want to vomit. And supposing I really had been dying? What then? What if I'd died today? What would you have done? (*She indicates the table laid for two*) Look! Look at it! The table is laid. For two. You would have sat down here while I was dead in that room and you would have eaten dinner with—that blood-sucking cow!

Domenico Am I not supposed to eat because you are dead? Would you like me to starve? To follow you into the grave?

Filumena There are roses on the table!

Domenico So there are roses on the table?

Filumena Red roses.

Domenico (*exasperated*) Red, green, blue, purple. If I want roses on the table when I'm eating, I will have roses on the table. What difference would roses on the table have made to you? You would have been lying dead. I'd have been more than happy to have put them on your coffin.

Filumena But I am not dead, Domenico—(*viciously*)—and I have no intention of dying for a long time.

Domenico So, we have this little problem. I'm baffled, you know, I really am. What was it you said I used to get? When I came to you? The same service as all the others? If you treated all men alike then—why not do it now? Find yourself one of the others and leave me alone. Why pick on me? And if I fall in love with another woman and I want to marry her—and I am going to marry Diana—what difference does it make to you if she is twenty-two years old or a hundred and twenty-two?

Filumena Marry her? Mother of God, I may not be able to cry but you make me laugh! I pity you. So you really think it matters to me what she is, who she is, where you found her, what you do with her. You really think that I've done all this because of you? A woman like me? Oh no, oh no. I do all this because I need you. There is something I need from you.

Domenico (*triumphantly*) Ah! Money. Why? Did you think I wouldn't have looked after you? Me, Domenico Soriano, son of Raimondo Soriano, one of the richest and most respected confectioners in Naples. So you really imagine that I would toss you out on to the streets without so much as a roof over your head. Have I ever argued over money?

Filumena Will you please be quiet about your money. You can keep your money and pile it up in the bank and good luck to you. It is something else I want from you and you are going to give it to me. I have three sons, Dummi'.

Domenico and Alfredo are dumbfounded. Rosalia is impassive

Domenico What's this—three sons? How do you mean, three sons?

Filumena I have three sons.

Domenico You are a childless woman—how can you suddenly have three sons?

Filumena I have three sons, Domenico.

Domenico You have no sons. You haven't even got a daughter. Where all at once can you produce three sons? Whose sons are they?

Filumena (*coldly, aware of his foreboding*) They are the sons of men like you.

Domenico Filume', what does that mean—"the sons of men like you?"

Filumena It means that all men are the same.

Domenico Watch what you're saying! You're playing a very dangerous game. Did you know this, Rosalia?

Rosalia (*carelessly, with a shrug*) Yes, that I knew.

Domenico (*to Alfredo*) How about you?

Alfredo How could I know it if you didn't? She hates me, you know!

Domenico (*still incredulous*) Three—sons? All boys?

Filumena All boys.

Domenico How old?

Filumena The eldest one is twenty-six.

Domenico Twenty-six . . . ?

Filumena Don't make that face. Don't be afraid. They are nothing to do with you.

Domenico Are you sure?

Filumena They are nothing to do with you.

Domenico Do they know they have a mother? I mean do they know who their mother is?

Filumena No. No, they don't know I am their mother—but I see them sometimes. I talk to them.

Domenico Explain it to me. They don't know that you're their mother—how do you see them? Where are they? What do they do? How do they live? Who brought them up?

Filumena You did.

Domenico Me?

Filumena Your money.

Domenico My money? What money?

Filumena It was your precious money. You've so much you didn't even know that it was going. I stole it from you. Over the years. Off your desk. Out of your pockets. Out of your wallet.

Domenico Thief!

Filumena Yes. Not only your money. Some of your suits. I sold them. Pairs of shoes. Things like that. Now and again a shirt. Cuff-links—tie-pins. Nothing too valuable but quite a lot, over a period of years. There was, of course, the diamond ring.

Domenico Which diamond ring?

Filumena Which diamond ring? The one with the big diamond. The one you thought you'd lost. You didn't lose it. I stole it. That was the only thing you ever noticed. But over twenty-five years I stole enough from you to provide for my three sons.

Domenico For twenty-five years I have harboured a thief under my roof. What kind of a woman are you? Do you feel no shame?

Filumena (*ignoring him*) One of them has his business premises just around the corner in the alley. He's a plumber.

Rosalia (*proudly*) No. He's a sanitary engineer.

Domenico A what?

Rosalia A sanitary engineer. Don't you know what a sanitary engineer is? He fixes pipes. Mends washers. He's the same as a plumber only more expensive. Then there's Riccardo. Such a handsome boy. The girls fight over him. He's a shirt-maker. Made-to-measure, you understand, not ready-to-wear. Well he owns a shop in the Via Chiaia, number seventy-four. Only the very best people go to him . . .

Domenico Really?

Rosalia Then, there is the third one, Umberto.

Filumena Umberto's the clever one. He's studied, passed his exams and became an accountant. He also writes pieces for the newspapers.

Domenico Ah? So we have got a writer in the family!

Rosalia Oh, and what a wonderful mother she has been to those boys. They never wanted for anything.

Domenico Really?

Rosalia No, it's true. Why should I lie? I'm an old woman. Very soon I'll be called to stand before our Supreme Being who sees and knows everything. How could I look Him in the face if I'd told a lie? If those children had asked for the milk of an ant she would have gone down on her hands and knees to get it for them. From the day each one of them came into this world—he has only had to ask, and it's been his.

Domenico What used to be mine.

Rosalia You have always had money to throw away.

Domenico Why not? Should I have asked your permission!

Rosalia Certainly not.

Filumena Don't listen to him. Why do you even bother to answer him?

Domenico Filumena, don't drive me too far! Do you realize what you have done? Now, on top of everything else, you suddenly announce that there are three men in the world that I've never even met, that I don't even know where they come from, who could be laughing at me, all this time, behind my back, and they'd be right to do so. They have been brought up by you to think whatever happens they can always go and screw old Domenico.

Rosalia No, no. They're not like that. You don't know them.

They've never known where the money comes from. Filumena
has a clever head on her shoulders. She did everything that had
to be done through a solicitor—very discreetly. He arranged the
money for the plumber to set himself up in business. He told the
boy the money came from a person who did not want her name
to be disclosed. And the same with Riccardo. And with the
monthly payments for Umberto to go on with his studies. You
had nothing to do with it.

Domenico No. No—I only provided the money.

Rosalie Exactly.

Domenico So the three bastards could make me the laughing-
stock of all Naples.

Filumena What would you have had me do? Kill them? Eh,
Dummi'? Do what all the other women in that brothel used to
do? Would that have made me a respectable woman? Go on,
answer me! "Get rid of it," they told me. "It's so easy—so
simple, Filumena." Would you have told me the same? Would
you have carried it in your conscience for the rest of your life?
Not me. I would rather have died myself than take the life of
one of those unborn children. And then, of course, I spoke to
the Madonna. The little Madonna of the Roses.

Rosalia The Madonna of the Roses—she performs a fresh
miracle every day of our life.

Domenico Oh please. Don't drag the Madonna into this mess.

Filumena Don't joke, Domenico. I'm telling you the truth. It
really happened. I found myself alone in the street. It was late
one night. I knew I was going to have a child. It was my first
time. What am I going to do? Who can I turn to? There is
no-one. I heard in my ears the buzzing voices of the other
women—my friends—in that house. "Get rid of it, Filumena."
"What are you waiting for?" "I know just the man that you
should go to." But I wouldn't listen to them. I walked and
walked and walked. All at once I found myself standing in the
street in front of the shrine of the Madonna of the Roses. I
stood there, looking up at her, like this. (*She stands, arms
akimbo, staring up*) You tell me: "What can I do? You know
everything—you know as well as I do why I'm living this
dreadful life. Tell me what to do." But she said nothing. "Why
don't you answer me?" Not a word. "I think I'm beginning to
understand," I said, "That is the way you people up there

operate—the less you talk, the more the ones down here be-
lieve in you. Is that it? I'm talking to you—answer—answer!"
And then I heard a voice: "A child is a child."
Domenico (*puzzled*) "A child is a child"?

*Both Rosalia and Alfredo shoot him warning glances—Rosalia
angrily; Alfredo because he is caught up in Filumena's story.
Domenico shrugs, mystified. Filumena has heard or seen none of
this*

Filumena "A child is a child." I was frozen to the spot. Like
stone. Perhaps if I'd turned round I would have seen or
understood where the voice had come from. From an open
window, perhaps, or someone standing on a balcony. But then
I thought—why—at this moment—did I get this answer? I
was the only one that knew that I was ... (*She pats her
stomach*) Those words were meant for me. That's the way she
chooses to speak to us—through other people. Then I
thought—when those other girls told me to get rid of it, that
was her, too, tempting me through them. As I stood there,
looking at her, I don't know if it was me or her who nodded.
It makes no difference. If it was me that nodded, it was her
nodding through me, to let me know she understood. "A
child is a child". I swore then—I made a vow. And because of
that vow I've put up with everything that you've done to me.
The way you've treated me—all these years. For them. For
the children. And when that young man fell in love with me
and wanted to marry me, do you remember? When you and I
had been together for five years—your wife was still alive
then, and I was living in that apartment where you put me
when you took me out of that house. He loved me so much,
that boy, he might even have accepted my children. But no,
all at once you were jealous. "I cannot marry you. If you leave
me for this boy I shall kill myself." And you started to cry.
You always knew how to cry. So I said good-bye to that poor
boy. Two years later, your wife died. And I went on living in
the apartment. I didn't press you. "No, give him time. He
knows the sacrifices you've made for him." So I waited. And I
waited. One day I said to you, "Dummi', do you know who's
just got married? The little girl you used to see playing in the
street. Married." And all you did was laugh. That arrogant

laugh of yours. The laugh I used to hear when you and your stupid friends were coming up the brothel stairs. I could have killed you when I heard that laugh. But I said nothing—and I waited. Twenty-five years I've waited and waited—for what? For him to start running around drooling over a twenty-two-year-old cow. Mother of God! But he is not putting her inside this house. (*Back to Domenico*) Try! Try! I warn you, try to put that cow inside this house now that I am your wife. I will throw her out. I will throw both you and her out. We are married. A priest married us. This house is mine.

The doorbell rings

Alfredo goes to answer it

Domenico bursts into laughter

Domenico Is this the laugh you were talking about? The laugh you didn't like to hear?

Filumena Go on—laugh—laugh. Don't worry. I like to hear you laugh now. It does not hurt any more. I enjoy hearing that laugh now, Dummi'. It's not quite so arrogant as it was before.

Alfredo returns, a little embarrassed at what he has to announce

Domenico What do you want?

Alfredo What do I want? The dinner's here.

Domenico All right. The dinner's here. What are you looking at your feet for? Aren't I supposed to eat?

Alfredo Of course! (*Calling off*) Bring it in!

Two restaurant Waiters enter, carrying covered dishes and a large box between them

First Waiter Good evening, Don Domenico. At your service, sir. (*To his colleague, indicating the table*) Put it down here.

The Waiters put the food down

(*Demonstrating*) I have brought you two small plump spring chickens. I am sure you will be well satisfied. Everything you ordered is just as you wanted it—top quality and extra-special service. Oh, sir, here is the dessert. I have managed to bring you the particular pudding that the young lady particularly enjoys.

Here's the wine, exactly as you ordered. I am sure you will be very satisfied. (*His words are met with a stony silence, but he does not seem to have noticed*) I have remembered everything—you haven't forgotten, have you, sir?

Domenico Forgotten what?

First Waiter What you said when you came to see me about the dinner, sir. I happened to enquire whether, perhaps, you might have an old pair of trousers you no longer had a use for. You said "If everything goes the right way, I'll give you a three-piece suit."

Domenico Get out.

The Waiter is upset

First Waiter Everything did not go the right way?
Domenico I told you to get out.

The Waiters leave

Filumena (*sarcastically*) Aren't you going to eat? Have you lost your appetite?
Domenico It's my meal—I'll eat and drink when I'm ready.

Diana enters from the front door. She is a snobbish woman about twenty-seven, trying to pass herself off as twenty-two. She looks down her nose at everybody. As she enters, she addresses the occupants of the room in general—as if there were certain present members of the company too much beneath her to be addressed in private. She has not noticed that Filumena is also there. She is carrying a basket with a number of small pharmaceutical parcels and a nurse's overall which she places on the table. She picks out the nurse's overall and slips it on

Diana Excuse me, Alfredo. (*To Domenico*) Oh, my dear, there was a time, at one point, when I thought I was going to have to stand in that chemist's for the entire evening. It was absolutely crowded to the doors. I'm exhausted. (*Peremptorily*) Run my bath, Rosalia, at once, please. (*She sees the roses on the table*) Red roses. How did you remember, Domenico? My favourite flowers. You're so sweet. You're spoiling me. The dinner smells good—I'm really famished. (*She takes out the pharmaceutical phials*) I brought the camphor and the adrenalin—but they were completely out of oxygen.

Domenico is rooted to the floor. Filumena has not batted an eyelid. Rosalia and Alfredo are amused by this turn of events

Do you know what crossed my mind while I was waiting in the chemist's? Domenico, I don't wish to speed a sad event, but if the poor woman "goes"—passes over—tonight, I shall leave first thing tomorrow morning. I'm not saying the wrong thing, am I? But if it's going to happen it's better it happens sooner than later. You won't want me around for a day or two. So I thought I'd keep out of the way for a while—how does that strike you? One's expected to show just a little respect. How is she? Has she finally taken a turn for the worse yet? Has the priest been sent for?

Filumena (*advancing on Diana*) The priest was sent for. The priest arrived. The priest stood in that room and testified to the evidence of my desperate condition. The priest said there was no hope for me. Take that thing off.

Diana What?

Filumena Take that thing off.

Diana is too stunned to take in the command. Rosalia demonstrates with her own apron

Rosalia Take off the overall that you are wearing.

Diana Oh!

Diana takes off the nurse's overall. Filumena watches her intently

Filumena (*pointing*) Put in on that chair.

Rosalia Place the overall on the chair.

Diana complies, and Filumena returns to her original theme. During the following, Diana, shocked beyond belief and unaware of what she is doing, picks up a rose from a vase on the table and toys with it

Filumena As I was saying, the priest recognized the agonized state I was in, so he therefore advised Don Domenico Soriano to legalize *in extremis* our sinful relationship . . . (*Furious again*) Put that rose back!

Diana What?

Filumena Put that rose back.

Rosalia In the vase.

Diana does as she is told

Filumena As I was saying, Don Domenico realized at once that what the priest was saying was only right and fair. "This poor woman," he said to himself, didn't you, Dummi'? "This poor woman has stood by me and given me twenty-five years of her life—of course I must marry her—I have no choice." So the plain truth of the matter is that Don Domenico and myself were married less than an hour ago while I was lying on my deathbed. Legally. With two witnesses. By the representative of the Holy Mother Church. Would you believe it—a wonderful recovery took place! Perhaps marriage is good for the health. Within seconds I was up and about. The funeral has been postponed. There is no illness in this house. It therefore follows that where there is no illness, there is no need for camphor and adrenalin, and no need for nurses.

Filumena strikes Diana on the chin with her index finger, making her head jerk from side to side

No filth. No cows. No farmyard animals. No filthy farmyard carrying on in front of a dying woman—because that's what you thought I was—a dying woman. So go away. Find somewhere else to bounce your tits and waggle your arse—there is no room for you in this house.

Diana (*with a fixed disbelieving grin on her face*) What does she mean, Domenico? (*She walks backwards towards the door*)

Filumena And if they can't accommodate you in the farmyard, go to the brothel I came from—I'm sure they'll find a place for you there.

Diana (*not comprehending*) Where?

Filumena Ask Don Domenico. He used to be a frequent visitor. He still frequents, I hear.

Diana (*panic-stricken*) Thank you.

Filumena Don't mention it.

Diana Good night!

Diana flees

Domenico, who has remained silent and bewildered throughout the above, now turns on Filumena

Domenico Did you have to treat the poor girl like that?

Filumena Poor girl? Cow! She got what she deserved.

Domenico Ah, forget the girl. There is something else going on in my mind. Something more important. You're a devil. You know that? It would be fatal to take one's eyes off you for a second. When you speak, every word has to be carefully noted and weighed one by one. I shall never understand you, but I admire you for what you are. You are like a spider. Some sort of poisonous spider weaving its web around its victim. You said something, and it has been going around and around in my head while you were abusing that poor girl. You said, "There is something else I want from you—and you're going to give it to me." This something else—what is it? I know it's not money. So what is it that you want from me? What is there going on in that mind that you haven't told me? Answer me! Come on, out with it.

Filumena Do you know that old song, Dummi'? (*She sings*) "I am teaching some tricks to a monkey. He is learning to do what I say."

Rosalia Mother of God!

Domenico Don't play the fool with me. Come on—out with it.

Filumena You are the monkey.

Domenico Filumena, don't talk in riddles. You drive me insane!

Filumena My sons are my sons.

Domenico For God's sake woman, say what you mean!

Filumena They must know who their mother is. They must know how much I love them—how much I need them to love me. It is not right that they should feel shame if someone asks to see their birth certificates. They should be part of one family. There should be someone there they can turn to for help. They must have the same name as me.

Domenico What name?

Filumena My name. I am married to you. Soriano.

Domenico (*passionately*) I knew it. All along I knew it, but I wanted to hear it from you, from that foul, blaspheming mouth of yours. So that I could convince myself that I would be in the right if I broke all your bones with my hands and crushed your skull into the ground with the heel of my shoe. It would be as right as crushing a snake. Here? Here? In my home? With my name? Those—those sons of—a—those sons of a . . .

Filumena Sons of a what? Say it! Say it!

Domenico Yours! Yours! Sons of yours. If you ask me sons of
   what, I can only answer—yours. If you ask me sons of whom, I
   cannot answer. Because I don't know. I don't know who their
   father is, and I'd be surprised if you could put a father's face
   to any of them. Bring three bastards into my house? I swear to
   you, Filumena, not one of them will put one foot inside this
   house, on my father's soul I swear it.

Filumena (*quietly, in earnest*) Don't swear, Domenico. I swore a
   vow once, and because of that vow, for twenty-five years I have
   been begging at your feet. Don't swear a vow you may not be
   able to keep. If you do you will die damned. One day you will
   have to break that vow and come begging at my feet.

Domenico What are you thinking now? You witch! But I am not
   afraid of you. You are not going to frighten me.

Filumena Why are you shouting then?

Domenico Shut up! (*He takes off his pyjama jacket*) Get me my
   jacket.

Alfredo goes into the study

   Tomorrow you will be out of this house—for good. I'll put
   everything in the hands of my lawyer. First thing tomorrow.
   I'll take you to court. You tried to trap me but you failed. I've
   got witnesses.

Filumena They were witnesses to a wedding. The law is on my
   side.

Domenico Pray that it isn't, Filumena. Pray. Because if the law
   finds for you—I will take the law in my own hands—I'll kill
   you with my hands, and that I do swear. I could pick you up,
   now—pick you up and throw you—throw you out of this
   world.

Filumena And where shall you put me?

Domenico (*switching on the lights*) Back in the whore-house—
   where you belong!

Alfredo returns with Domenico's jacket

Domenico snatches the jacket from him and puts it on

   Tomorrow morning you're to get my solicitor, do you understand?

Alfredo nods

Then we'll talk, Filume'.

Filumena All right. We'll talk then.

Domenico You'll find out that Don Domenico Soriano is not the fool you thought he was!

Domenico moves upstage, on his way out

Filumena (*indicating the dinner on the table*) Rosalia, it's such a pity to waste this food. Sit down. You must be hungry too.

Rosalia sits down at the table

Domenico Enjoy yourself, Filumena de Napolitana.

Filumena (*singing*) I am teaching some tricks to a monkey: he is learning to do what I say.

As Filumena starts to sing, Domenico laughs at her, insultingly

Domenico Remember this laugh, Filumena Marturano? Remember it well.

Domenico storms out, followed by Alfredo, as—

the CURTAIN *falls*

ACT II

The same. The following day, a bright, sunny morning

Lucia, the maid, has cleared away the chairs in order to wash the floor. Some of the chairs are out on the terrace, others are upside-down on the table. Lucia is a healthy, good-natured girl in her early twenties. She has just finished washing the floor and is wringing out the floor-cloth in a bucket of water. Having done this, she puts her cleaning things away out on the terrace. As she returns to the living-room and begins to put back the furniture, Alfredo enters from the outer door, looking tired

Alfredo Good morning, Lucia.
Lucia Stand still!

Alfredo stops dead in his tracks

Don't move. Don't you walk across the floor with your big feet!
Alfredo What shall I do? Walk on my hands? (*He sits on the settee*)
Lucia Can't you see I've just finished washing that floor. It's still wet. And you walk in with those great, big clumping feet of yours! (*She replaces the chairs, paying him scant attention*)
Alfredo It's not just my feet that are clumping. My head is clumping too. I've been out all night with Don Domenico. Wandering around. I haven't laid my head down for a second. Half the night was spent sitting on a bench on the seafront at Caracciolo. Mother of God, I thought I was going to freeze to death! I'm not complaining, don't think that. Don Domenico has been very good to me. I hope he lives a thousand years— but please God let him lead a quiet, ordered life. I'm too old for these carryings-on. Lucia, please, do me a favour, bring me some coffee.
Lucia There isn't any coffee.
Alfredo Didn't Rosalia make some this morning?
Lucia No.

Alfredo Why?

Lucia She went out at the crack of dawn.

Alfredo Where to?

Lucia I don't know. All she said was that she had three important letters to be written on behalf of Donna Filumena and delivered by hand.

Alfredo *Three* letters? Three!

Lucia *Three* letters—after two and before four, you know? Three.

Alfredo (*overwhelmed by fatigue*) If I don't get a cup of coffee soon I'm a dead man. Please, Lucia, some coffee.

Lucia All right. I'll make you some and bring it to you.

Lucia exits to the kitchen as Rosalia enters through the outer door

Alfredo Don't you even say "good morning", Rosalia?

Rosalia I didn't see you sitting there.

Alfredo You didn't see me? What did you think I was? Part of the furniture? Where've you been?

Rosalia To Mass, of course. Where do you think?

Alfredo Oh! To Mass! You wouldn't have had time to deliver Donna Filumena's letters, then?

Rosalia If you knew where I'd been, why did you ask me?

Alfredo Because I wanted to see if you would tell me. I thought it might be a secret.

Rosalia I don't keep secrets.

Alfredo Who were the letters for?

Rosalia Mind your own business.

Alfredo "I don't keep secrets." "Mind your own business."

Rosalia It's true I don't keep secrets. On the other hand, I don't tell everything to people with loose tongues.

Alfredo You don't mean me?

Rosalia Yes. You. One of these days your tongue will drop off. What's more, it won't be long before you lose your nose too—it spends far too much time in other people's business.

Alfredo What! Oh! When? (*He rises*) When have I ever poked my nose in your affairs?

Rosalia I didn't say mine—I said "other people's". I haven't got any affairs. My life is an open book. It's common knowledge. (*She launches into a monologue*) I was born into a poor

family, seventy-five years ago. Everybody knows that. My
mother was a washerwoman. My father was a blacksmith. My
husband and I were joined together in holy matrimony on the
second day of November, nineteen hundred. It rained all the
day we got married. But that was a good sign.

Alfredo A good sign?

Rosalia My husband used to repair umbrellas. Our union was
blessed with three children—all at once. Triplets. The midwife
rushed round to my husband's workshop with the happy news.
He had a little shop just around the corner. She found him with
his head in the sink . . .

Alfredo He was washing his face?

Rosalia No. It's not funny. At the very moment that his three
children came into the world, their father had had a heart attack
and left it. Imagine this poor orphan child . . .

Alfredo *Three* poor orphan children?

Rosalia *One* poor orphan child.

Alfredo One?

Rosalia Me. One. Both my parents were gone. How could they
be orphans? Their mother was still alive, wasn't I? Idiot.
Sit down.

Alfredo sits

I was alone in the world with three hungry mouths crying out
for bread. So I took a couple of rooms in the Via San Liborio
and set up in business for myself. I sold fly-swatters, remem-
brance candles for the dead, and party hats for festive oc-
casions. We got by—only just—but I managed to feed and
clothe my three children. It was in those days I first met
Donna Filumena—when she was a little girl. She used to play
in the street with my three boys. When the boys grew up they
all emigrated. There was no work here, so off they went. One
to Australia, one to the United States, and one to . . .

Alfredo Argentina.

Rosalia No, no. Yes, you're right—Argentina. Have I told you
this story before? I never saw them again. There I was, a
middle-aged woman, nothing left only memories. If it hadn't
been for the good heart of Donna Filumena, who brought me
with her when she moved in with Don Domenico, I would have
been starving in the street: a beggar sitting on the steps of a

church. That's the end of the story. Thank you for your kind
attention.

Rosalia exits to the bedroom

Alfredo (*rising and calling*) Lucia!
Lucia (*off*) All right, I'm coming.

*Lucia enters with a cup of coffee, but as she is about to hand it to
Alfredo, Domenico enters from the outer door*

Domenico Is that coffee?
Lucia (*looking at Alfredo, helplessly*) Good morning, Don
Domenico.

*Domenico takes the cup from Lucia and drains it at a gulp. He
hands her back the empty cup*

Domenico Thanks. I needed that!
Alfredo So did I.
Domenico Was it for you? I'm sorry.

Lucia goes out to the kitchen

Did you go to the solicitor's?
Alfredo Yes, straight away. As soon as I left you.
Domenico Did he say when he could get here?
Alfredo As quickly as he can get away.
Domenico When's that?
Alfredo Whenever he's dealt with his appointments.
Domenico So when is that going to be?
Alfredo Today, at any rate.
Domenico (*voicing his thoughts*) Can anything be done about this
awful mess? What if the solicitor says that she is right, that the
law's the law, that I don't stand a cat in hell's chance. What
about the church. We were married in front of a priest, weren't
we, Alfredo?

*Alfredo's thoughts are elsewhere. He drags them back to the
present*

Alfredo Yes, a priest.
Domenico What can I do, then? Why do I bother to confide in
you? I'm wasting my time. I must be crazy. (*Looking at him,*

suddenly, with new eyes—kindly) What happened to you, Alfredo Amoroso?

Alfredo What happened to me?

Domenico You're an old man. Your hair's turned white, you're a bag of bones, your face is creased, your eyesight's going— now you're going soft in the head!

Alfredo (*never one to contradict his master*) By God, you're right!

Domenico (*realizing that he, himself, is no longer young*) The years rush past. Alfredo, for all of us. Do you remember Don Domenico Soriano?

Alfredo (*not understanding—but pretending to*) Of course, of course! What happened to him? Is he dead?

Domenico (*sadly*) Yes. He's dead. Stone dead. Don Domenico Soriano is well and truly dead—he is not in his grave, that's all.

Alfredo Ah, you mean this Domenico Soriano.

Domenico The black moustache I used to have. The hard, flat belly. I slept with so many women, eh, I don't believe that I ever slept at all!

Alfredo (*yawning*) Good times!

Domenico Do you remember that girl, the one at the Café Monte, the body on her? Christ! What I gave to her! I really roasted that one! And what about the vet's wife?

Alfredo The vet's wife! That's right. I *do* remember her! She was the one that had the sister-in-law that I was chasing—I never got anywhere. We never found anything to say to each other.

Domenico And the horses we rode? Do you remember riding down to the Villa together?

Alfredo You looked like a God in the saddle!

Domenico I had that grey suit. A hard hat and a silk scarf. And the horses—all the best horses belonged to me. Silver Eyes, do you remember her?

Alfredo Remember her? She was my favourite. A backside like a full moon. Do I remember her? I was in love with that horse She was more to me than any woman.

Domenico (*lost in memories*) Paris. London. How we travelled. Travel and horses. I *was* a God, Alfredo. I owned the world. No man ever gave me an order. I was Don Domenico Soriano then—and the mountains were mine and the sea was mine and I belonged only to myself. What has happened to that man, Alfredo? What has become of that Don Domenico Soriano? It's as if I'm finished—no urge—no drive—no love of life. But I'm still that same man, aren't I, that I used to be? I feel that I have to prove it to myself—and I will prove it—I still have that strength. Don Domenico will face death before defeat.

Filumena enters from her bedroom. She is wearing a housecoat and her hair is in disarray. Rosalia is with her and is carrying some bed-linen. Filumena ignores Domenico and Alfredo

Filumena (*calling*) Lucia! (*To Rosalia*) Give me the keys.
Rosalia Here they are.

Filumena puts the bunch of keys in the pocket of her housecoat and waits impatiently for Lucia

Filumena Where is that girl! (*Louder*) Lucia!

Lucia enters

Lucia Here, signora!
Filumena Take these sheets.

Rosalia hands the linen to Lucia

The sofa in the little sitting-room next to the study, I want you to make it up into a bed.
Lucia (*amazed*) Into a *bed*, signora?

Lucia moves to leave but Filumena stops her

Filumena Wait a moment. I need your bed as well.
Lucia (*more amazed*) My bed as well?
Filumena There are enough sheets there for two beds—make yourself up somewhere to sleep in the kitchen.
Lucia (*even more amazed*) In the kitchen, signora?
Filumena I need your room.
Lucia What about all my things, signora? Can I leave them in the chest of drawers?
Filumena Take them out—I need your chest of drawers as well.

Lucia goes out through the hall, aggrieved

Filumena pretends that she has just seen Domenico

Domenico Excuse me. Am I allowed to know what's happening in my own house?

Filumena Certainly. There should not be any secrets between husband and wife. I need two more bedrooms.

Domenico Am I allowed to know who for?

Filumena For my sons.

Domenico Only two?

Filumena That's all. It would have been three, but one of them is married with four children. He has his own family to look after.

Domenico Good! Grandchildren as well! It's good to know they're legitimate! And what's the name of this tribe dropping in on us?

Filumena It's not important—they'll be changing it to yours as soon as you give them your permission.

Domenico Never!

Filumena Oh, you'll give it!

Domenico I'll see the bastards in hell first!

Filumena No, Dummi'—you'll agree to it. Before I have finished you'll say "yes".

Filumena goes off to the bedroom

Rosalia (*with mocking servility*) Excuse me, please, Don Domenico.

Rosalia follows Filumena

Domenico calls to Filumena through the open door

Domenico They will not set foot in this house! Do you understand that? I will slam the door in their faces . . .

At which point, the door through which Filumena has just gone through is slammed in Domenico's face

Lucia enters

Lucia Don Dummi', Signorina Diana is outside. She has brought a gentleman with her.

Domenico Don't leave her on the doorstep. Ask her to come in.

Lucia I did ask her to come in. She says she doesn't want to. She says, will you go out to her? I think she's frightened of Donna Filumena.

Domenico Does she think I am not master in my own house? Will you tell them to come in. In here.

Lucia Very good, signor.

Lucia goes out

Alfredo If Donna Filumena sets eyes on her—(*he draws his finger across his throat*)—she'll really finish her this time.

Domenico (*raising his voice so that Filumena can hear him*) Whatever is to be finished, will be finished by me! I say who comes and goes. Only me! (*Alluding to Filumena*) She is nothing here! What I say goes!

Lucia returns

Lucia Don Dummi', she says, if it's all the same to you, she'd still rather stay outside. She says, if she did come in, she couldn't be responsible for her temper.

Domenico Her what?

Lucia Her temper.

Domenico Who is it she's brought with her?

Lucia Her solicitor.

Domenico Her solicitor?

Lucia I think he's frightened as well.

Domenico Frightened of what? With us two, that would make three men in here.

Alfredo No. Don't count on me for anything this morning—last night nearly finished me. I'd be no use at all. You won't want me around anyway—you'll want to talk. I'm going to have a wash—see if I can wake myself up. If you want me, I'll be in the kitchen.

Domenico What sort of a friend are you?

Alfredo goes out to the kitchen without waiting for an answer

Lucia What do you want me to do, Don Dummi'?

Domenico Nothing. I'll go myself.

Lucia goes off to the kitchen. Domenico goes off to the outer door. He returns a moment or two later, ushering in Diana and the solicitor, Nocella

Domenico You've got nothing to worry about—this is my house.

Diana (*hovering in the doorway, nervously*) I'm extremely sorry,

Domenico. I do not want to see that—that woman again,
face to face—it wouldn't be fair to you—I couldn't count
myself responsible for my actions.

Domenico Diana, come on! Don't make a fool of me. There's
nothing to be afraid of, I promise you.

Diana Afraid? Me? Afraid of—her? Let me assure you Domenico, that I know very well how to handle women of her kind.
But I'd rather not, if it's all the same to you. I don't want to
lose my temper.

Domenico You won't have to lose your temper. I'm here to deal
with the situation.

Diana You were here last night.

Domenico Last night I wasn't ready for it. Today, I am prepared
for anything. Signor—er . . .

Nocella Nocella. Pasquale Nocella.

Domenico Please, Signor Nocella, make yourself at home.

Diana Where is she?

Domenico It's not important. Somewhere in the house. It doesn't
matter. Please, sit down.

*The three of them sit down around the dining-table. Nocella sits in
the middle. Diana's eyes are glued fearfully, on the door of the
bedroom*

(*Encouragingly*) Signor Nocella, you are a solicitor. This is
very good.

*Nocella is an ordinary, insignificant man of about forty. He is
wearing a dark suit and neat collar and tie. He has been talked into
the Soriano affair by Diana, and seems reluctant to be involved*

Nocella Signorina Diana and I share the same lodgings—it's a
small private hotel, she's probably told you.

Domenico No.

Diana Signor Nocella can tell you what kind of woman I am and
what kind of life I lead.

Nocella We see each other across the dinner table in the evenings
though I am not there for dinner very often. You know my
work, courts, clients. And besides I'm not the kind of man who
looks to get involved with people. I prefer to keep myself to
myself.

Diana's fears about the possibility of the sudden appearance of Filumena are growing, visibly

Diana Excuse me, Domenico—would you mind if you sat here and I sat there?
Domenico No. By all means.

Domenico and Diana change seats. Diana continues what Nocella was saying

Diana So! It was at dinner last night that I was telling Signor Nocella about your trouble with Filumena.
Nocella Yes, yes—we fell about laughing!

Domenico frowns at Diana

Diana No. Not me. I didn't think it at all funny.

Nocella glances at her, knowingly

Domenico You see, Signor Nocella, Diana has often been here recently and because of certain circumstances. I asked her to pretend to be a nurse.
Diana But I am a nurse.
Domenico You are a nurse?
Diana I have a certificate to prove it. Didn't I tell you that, Domenico?
Domenico No. You never mentioned it to me.
Diana Strange? I thought I had. (*Returning to the matter in hand*) I was telling Signor Nocella last night about your problems. How worried you were. He was explaining the law to me—he went into it very fully . . .

The doorbell rings. Domenico starts

Domenico What's that?

Lucia enters and goes to answer the door

Lucia (*as she crosses the room*) The front door, signor.
Domenico Shall we move into the study? We will be less likely to be disturbed there.
Diana (*rising*) Perhaps we should.

Domenico shows Diana and Nocella into the study

Domenico This way.
Nocella (*going first*) Thank you.

Nocella exits

Domenico How do we stand? What does he say?
Diana Better he tells you. (*She strokes his cheek*) Poor Domenico—you're as white as a ghost!

*Diana goes into the study, followed by Domenico. Lucia ushers
in Umberto*

Lucia In here—please, sit down.

*Umberto is a tall, well-built but studious young man. His straight-
forward manner, coupled with his habit of closely observing people,
is inclined to embarrass them*

Umberto Thank you.
Lucia Over there, please. I don't know when Donna Filumena
will see you.
Umberto That's quite all right. I'll be fine here. (*He sits down on
the settee and starts scribbling in a notebook he has brought with
him*)

Lucia starts to go to the bedroom but the doorbell rings again

*Lucia exits to answer the bell, and a moment later ushers in
Riccardo*

Lucia In here—please, sit down.

*Riccardo is a charming young man, elegantly dressed. He enters
looking at his wrist watch*

Riccardo This isn't going to take all day, is it? I run a business.
If the boss isn't there, the staff stand around and twiddle their
thumbs.
Lucia (*impressed*) You have your own business?

Riccardo shrugs, over-modestly

How many people work there?
Riccardo Me and another fellow. Hey! Where are you going?
Lucia I am the staff. My boss is in the other room. I've got to
scrub the kitchen floor.

Riccardo You shouldn't be scrubbing floors with a face like yours!

Lucia I don't, signor, I use a scrubbing-brush.

Riccardo Don't joke. I mean it. You should be a model or an actress.

Lucia Go away.

Riccardo Really—the next time you're passing, call in and see me at my shop.

Lucia (*impressed*) You own a shop?

Riccardo (*shrugging, modestly*) Number seventy-four, in the Via Chiaia. Drop in. Anytime. I'll slip a tape-measure round you.

Lucia Is it a dress shop?

Riccardo No—not really—it's a menswear shop. I sell ties and caps and I make men's shirts.

Lucia Oh? That's not the shop for me.

Riccardo I could make you a shirt.

Lucia Are you mad? Do you want to put me in a man's shirt? Go away.

Riccardo No—listen—I serve both men and women. I put shirts on men and take them off women. (*He makes a grab at her*)

Lucia Stop it! I may look like an actress but I don't behave like one. If you take one step further forward I'll tell the signora.

He makes another grab at her, and she calls out in a very low voice

Signora! (*Indicating Umberto*) Don't you know there's some-body watching?

Riccardo I didn't know we had an audience. (*To Umberto*) Hello. How are you?

Lucia You don't know anything. You got me wrong, too.

Riccardo I'll get to know you better. When are you coming to see me at the shop?

Lucia Number seventy-four?

Riccardo Number seventy-four. When are you coming?

The doorbell rings

Lucia Wait and see.

Lucia goes off, giving Riccardo a broad smile

Riccardo walks up and down the room. He looks across at Umberto, who is still watching him, and feels that he needs to justify his behaviour

Riccardo She's nice that one, Half an hour with her and you'd know about it, eh?

Umberto Yes. (*Shrugging*) She's all right.

Riccardo She's more than all right—what are you, a priest, or is there something wrong with you?

Umberto I beg your pardon? (*He goes back to scribbling in his notebook*)

Lucia (*off*) Through here, Michele.

Lucia ushers in Michele. He is a plump young man in blue overalls. He carries a plumber's bag of tools

Michele What is it this time, Luci'? Not the tap on the bath again? I only put a new washer on it last week.

Lucia There's nothing wrong with the bath.

Michele The waste-pipe under the kitchen sink's clogged up— I'll tell Donna Filumena what you've been doing with your tea-leaves!

Lucia You tell her. I'll go and fetch her for you. (*She goes to the door and pauses*) We don't have tea-leaves, because everybody in this house drinks coffee. There's nothing wrong with the waste-pipe under the kitchen sink.

Lucia pulls a face at Michele and goes out. Michele smiles at Umberto

Michele Good morning.
Umberto Good morning.

Riccardo inclines his head in a peremptory acknowledgement.

Michele takes a half-smoked cigarette from behind his ear

Have you got a light?

Riccardo No, I haven't.

Michele Never mind. (*He puts the cigarette away again*) I haven't seen you here before. You're not a relative, are you? Are you waiting to see somebody?

Riccardo What are you? A plumber, or a private detective?

Michele What do you mean?

Riccardo You're the kind of man that likes to talk. I don't like to talk. I don't have the time to talk.

Michele There's no need to get nasty. I only asked a civil question.

Riccardo I'm giving you a civil answer. You take care of your blocked-up sinks and your bath-tap washers. I'll look after my own affairs.

Michele Excuse me—I didn't know I was talking to God Almighty.

Umberto He's not God Almighty—just a very rude man.

Riccardo What's wrong with you?

Umberto I'm sorry, but you are. You walked in here, to someone else's home, as if you owned the place. You try to make it with the maid—

Riccardo Of course . . .

Umberto—you get the cold shoulder there so you try to insult me.

Riccardo I never did.

Umberto You did! You did! Now this poor fellow walks in, and you treat him like a piece of dirt.

Michele Who are you calling a poor fellow? Thanks all the same, but I'll handle my own arguments. You keep out of it.

Umberto Okay, okay.

Michele (*rounding on Riccardo*) You be careful how you speak to people. Politeness costs nothing. And it's better than losing all your teeth. It's lucky for you we're guests in someone's house.

Riccardo Oh, shut up—you bore me.

Michele lets his tool-bag drop to the floor

Michele Say that again.

Riccardo Certainly. You bore me. You're an ignorant pig. I don't care if we are in somebody else's house—I'll knock your teeth out just the same.

Michele beckons Riccardo towards him, impudently

Michele Come on. Try me. Try me. I dare you.

Riccardo Don't force me to do it—I can't be bothered.

Michele Go away before I spoil the crease in your trousers for you, you tailor's dummy.

Riccardo That's it! That's enough! Who are you calling a tailor's dummy?

Michele Who are you calling an ignorant pig?
Riccardo I asked you first. Who are you calling a tailor's dummy?

Riccardo squares up his fists and advances in what he thinks is the style of a professional boxer. Michele waits for him without offering any form of defence. As Riccardo approaches him, Michele points to an imaginary mark on his tie

Michele What's that there?

Riccardo, puzzled, glances down at his tie, as he does so, Michele jerks up his hand, catching Riccardo under the nose. Riccardo's pride is stung. He takes a clumsy swing at Michele but Umberto has moved towards them and he grabs at Riccardo's arm

Umberto What are you doing?

Riccardo struggles to free himself from Umberto's grip. Michele too tries to force Umberto away. The three of them engage in a half-hearted brawl in which kicks and slaps and punches are aimed, but none of them seem to find their mark. The three men are far more proficient, it seems, with oaths and insults which they hurl at each other, than they are with blows. The scuffle is finally brought to a close by the arrival of Filumena

   Filumena enters, followed by Rosalia

Filumena Stop it! Stop it, do you hear? Where do you think you
   are? In the street? In the square? This is my home!

The three men are shame-faced

Umberto I wasn't fighting—I was trying to separate them.
Riccardo So was I.
Michele And me.
Filumena And who was doing the fighting?
Riccardo
Michele } They were (*Speaking together*)
Umberto
Filumena Terrible! You ought to be ashamed—one against the
   other!

The men shuffle their feet, embarrassed. Filumena pauses, not sure how to continue

   (*At last*) How is everything?

Michele Not bad—thank God.

Filumena Are the children well?

Michele Not bad. Dorino, the eldest boy, gave his mother another grey hair last week. While she was busy in the bedrooms he went into the kitchen and ate four pounds of grapes all by himself. The poor kid was in agony. (*He holds his hands out in front of his stomach, demonstrating*) His belly was out here.

Filumena Did you send for the doctor?

Michele Doctors! Hospitals! Two big spoonfuls of castor oil. It cures everything. The only trouble was, with my kids, whatever one gets—the others want the same thing too. Even castor oil.

Umberto Ah, now I remember, signora, when I got your letter this morning I hadn't the faintest idea who it was from, because I never knew your name. You are Donna Filumena! I used to see you almost every evening when I was on my way to the newspaper offices. I had the great pleasure of helping you home once—here—when you had stumbled and sprained your ankle . . .

Filumena That's right. You held my arm all the way.

Riccardo Excuse me, I'm a very busy man. What's all this about?

Filumena Are things going well at the shop?

Riccardo Why shouldn't they go well? The only time they go bad is when you come in—if all my customers were like you I'd be bankrupt in a fortnight. (*To the others*) I have to take down every roll of cloth on the shelves. "Not this one, I want a finer weave. Not this one, I want pure cotton not a mixture." (*Back to Filumena*) When you finally decide to leave it isn't a shop any longer—it's a disaster area.

Filumena (*motherly*) If you'd rather I didn't come into the shop, all right. I'll stay away.

Riccardo No, please! No. A customer's a customer. If you run a shop you learn to take the rough with the smooth. You come in whenever you want. But please, tell me, today, why have I had to come to you?

Umberto Yes, and why me, too?

Michele And me, too. Lucia says there's nothing wrong with the bathroom tap this time.

Filumena You are all three here for the same important reason.

(She indicates the terrace door) If you'll come through here on the terrace we'll be more comfortable.

Domenico enters from the study, followed by Nocello. Domenico is confident and self-assured. He speaks to Filumena not unkindly

Domenico I think it would be better if you didn't go through there. Even without being a lawyer, I knew I was right all along. Everything was so clear. Now, this gentleman here *is* a lawyer. Signor Nocella.

Filumena looks at Nocella dubiously

He will tell you everything you need to know about the situation. *(To the Three Sons)* The signora made a mistake. She's sorry that she dragged you round here without cause. We apologize, and now if you would like to leave . . .

The Three Sons, puzzled, turn to go

Filumena No. Stay. I did not make a mistake. I asked them to come round here. I have got something I wish to tell them. This is my business—it is nothing to do with you!

Domenico Filumena, what happens in this house is my affair. Must we discuss our private business in front of strangers?

It is Domenico's calm tones rather than his words that convince Filumena that things are not going the way she planned. She speaks to the Three Sons

Filumena Excuse me, please—would you mind waiting on the terrace for just five minutes?

Umberto and Michele exchange a puzzled glance and move to do as they have been told. But they pause as Riccardo looks at his watch

Riccardo No, I am sorry—but no. You really are asking too much of people. I have a business to attend to.

Filumena *(losing her temper; as if to a child)* Don't argue with me! If I tell you to wait on the terrace with your—with the others, you'll do as you're told!

Riccardo joins Umberto and Michele

(To Rosalia) Take them out some coffee.

Rosalia Come along. Be a good boy. (*To the Three Sons*) Do what she tells you. (*Showing them the way*) Rosalia will make you a beautiful cup of coffee.

Rosalia leads Umberto, Michele and Riccardo out on to the terrace

Filumena (*to Domenico*) Well? What have you got to say?

Domenico Here's the lawyer—talk to him.

Filumena I don't trust lawyers. (*To Nocella*) They are all out to help themselves first. Go on—say what you have to say.

Nocella Signora, I want you to know first that I have got nothing to do with this at all.

Filumena No? Then what are you doing here?

Nocella What I mean is, that I am not being employed to act on behalf of Signor Soriano. He did not send for me.

Filumena You mean you came here of your own accord?

Nocella No! No!

Filumena Nobody sent for you, but you didn't come here of your own accord. You have only said two things and they don't make sense.

Domenico For God's sake let him speak. At least listen to what he has to say.

Filumena Go on!

Nocella The plain truth of the matter, signora, if you will let me explain it to you fully, is that I was not summoned here by Signor Soriano—nor did I take it upon myself to arrive—in actual point of fact, I was *brought* here by the signorina. (*He looks around and realizes that Diana is not present*)

Domenico It's not important how you got here . . .

But Filumena has realized what has happened

Filumena Her? The cow's here again, is she? In there. (*Loudly*) I don't blame her if she's afraid to come out! Carry on, please.

Nocella I am not fully conversant with all the finer details, you understand? I have already explained that I am not officially engaged to act on anyone's behalf on this case, but as I see it, to me—or rather, as she's explained it to me—well, appertaining to the Laws of Court, Article one hundred and one, which, for all our benefits, I have looked up. (*He takes a book from* *his case*) Article one hundred and one. Which refers to the law regarding a Marriage which has been entered into when the life of one or other of the contractual partners of that marriage etcetera, etcetera is in mortal danger. Now then, in the case of such a marital union where one of the participants in the marriage contract, be it the husband or the wife etcetera, etcetera is in danger of losing his life in the case of the husband, or her life in the case of the wife, etcetera etcetera, that contract may be considered legal and binding—except, as I understand your particular circumstance, it may *not* be considered legal and binding as nobody's life *was* in mortal danger at the time that the marriage contract was entered into. As at the time that the marriage *was* entered into, the mortal danger referred to was all a fake. And, according to Article one hundred and one, Laws of Court, your marriage is *void ab unitio*.

Filumena (*genuinely*) I have not understood one word of what he has said.

Domenico (*who also has not understood, but has no wish to say so*) It's perfectly simple and straightforward. He is telling you exactly what I told you last night. I married you only because you promised me you were going to die.

Nocella No, no, no, no, no! You haven't taken my point at all. According to the law, under circumstances such as those, you couldn't even marry her. You cannot subject a marriage to conditions. There is a specific Article of Law that covers that exact contingency. Article one hundred and forty-seven—or is it one-seventy-four?—the number's not important. But the particular article states that if the two contractual parties add any limitation or condition, etcetera, etcetera, the registrar, or priest, whichever may be applicable, etcetera, etcetera, cannot proceed with the wedding ceremony.

Domenico Explain to her again the article where it says about marrying in mortal danger, etcetera etcetera.

Filumena What do you know about it? You understand no more than I do. I would like to hear it in plain simple language.

Nocella Signora, it is here in black and white. And here is the document. It is irrefutable. You can read it for yourself.

Filumena I can't read. (*Indicating Domenico*) He knows I can't read. And I don't touch papers.

Nocella It's very simple. Signora, since your life was not in danger at the time of the wedding, then the marriage is annulled.

Filumena Annulled?

Nocella Not valid. It never existed.

Filumena I was married by a priest. It was a priest that joined us together.

Nocella Go to that priest and he will tell you exactly the same as me. Your marriage is not valid. He would go further—you have committed sacrilege.

Domenico Good, good, good.

Filumena Not valid? Supposing I had died? I had to die?

Nocella Ah! In that case . . . Exactly!

Filumena Exactly what? What if I had died?

Nocella Of course, that would have been perfectly satisfactory. You would have entered into a legal marriage.

Filumena indicates Domenico, who has remained calm through all of the above

Filumena And if I had died, he could have married again? He could have had children?

Nocella Certainly. He would have been a widower. The next lucky lady of his choice would have married the widower of the late Signora Filumena Soriano.

Domenico If you had died you could have been Signora Soriano without any argument at all.

Filumena Thank you very much. And thank you too, Signor Nocella. So I spent my whole life trying to bring together one family, and the Law won't let me. And that's what you call Justice?

Nocella But my dear lady, you cannot twist the Law to suit your ends. Even if from a human point of view it might seem justified. Not if, by doing so, you seek to hurt or damage another party. Domenico Soriano does not wish to be your husband.

Domenico That's all there is to it. And if you don't believe us call any lawyer you like. They'll all tell you the same thing.

Filumena No, I don't need to call any lawyer. I believe it. Not because you say so, and not because he says so either. But I can tell it's true just by looking at your face, Domenico. You don't think I don't know you well enough? Yes, it's true.

You've got that look again. It says it in your eyes—you've won—you're the boss. I believe it—we're not married.

Domenico Good. We've got that straight at last. Signor Nocella, can you draw up the necessary documents to complete the formalities?

Nocella If you wish me to act on your behalf—and if I also have the Signora's permission?

Filumena does not reply for some moments

Filumena (*suddenly, as if making up her mind*) Yes. You have it. If he doesn't want me—I don't want him. Yes, it's true I was not about to die. And yes, it's true that I tried to trick him. But not because I wanted him for a husband—all I wanted was to steal his name. I don't care what your law says. (*Striking her breast*) I only know the law that is here. The law that teaches people not to cry—not the one that makes them laugh. I know, in here, what is right—and what I have to do. (*She calls to the Three Sons out on the terrace*) Hey, you! Come in! At once!

Domenico Filumena, will you please stop!

Filumena Shut up!

Umberto, Michele and Riccardo enter from the terrace: Riccardo is finishing a cup of coffee. Rosalia follows them. Realizing the seriousness of the moment, she moves to Filumena's side, attentively

Listen to me. You are three grown men and I can be frank and honest with you. (*Indicating Domenico and Nocella*) You see, these two, they are men of the world. The world with all its laws and its rights and its etceteras. The world which protects and defends itself with paper and ink. That's Domenico Soriano and that's a lawyer—and here is me—Filumena Marturano—whose only law is the law of those who cannot cry. Domenico Soriano will tell you that—he has never, once, seen a tear in my eye. So now—without crying—and you see my eyes, they are dry——

Domenico Filumena . . .

Filumena —I tell you that you are my three children.

Domenico Filumena—Filumena . . .

Filumena Who are you to try to stand between me and my own three sons? Who are you to tell me that I cannot tell them who they are? They are my children. Signor Nocella, there is no etcetera, is there, that says I must not tell my children that I am their mother? No—you are my three sons and I am Filumena Marturano. Well—you are three grown men and you may have heard people talk about me?

Umberto, Riccardo and Michele stand stock-still, as if struck dumb. Umberto's face is drawn, Riccardo's eyes are downcast, while Michele looks childishly surprised and emotional

In general, when people slander other people, they lie: in my case they were right. I was a whore. I was a whore when I was seventeen. (*Pause*) Signor Nocella, do you know the slums at San Giovanni, at Vergini, at Forcella, at Atribunale, at San Liborio? Filth and smoke and the awful stink of too many people living in one room? What do you think it was like in the summers, when the heat was so bad you could hardly breathe? Or in the winter, in the middle of the night, when you are twelve years old and your belly is empty and there are no bedclothes? How do you think a girl of thirteen feels when she has to share a bed with three brothers and a sister? Or to be fourteen and growing up and not even a pair of shoes? That was me. That was where I came from, a slum at San Liborio. It had three rooms. There were so many of us that if I try to remember, I lose count. I can only remember that we were always hungry. Angry, hungry, thin faces with nothing to say to each other. We went to bed without saying "good night". We got up without saying "good morning". I only ever remember anybody ever smiling at me once. That was my father. I was fifteen then, and still I grow cold when I think about it. "You've grown into a fine-looking girl, Filumena, and there's not a thing to eat in the house." We used to sit round the dinner table with only one bowl of food in the middle and so many forks. After that, whenever I put my fork in that bowl I felt them all looking at me as if I was stealing the food from their mouths. And how stifling it was when we had to close the door at night! Some nights I would stand outside and watch other girls go by. Girls with frocks that nobody but themselves had worn, good shoes on their feet, smart handbags. One night I met a girl I had known as a child. She was so well-dressed that I didn't recognize her at first. When you are seventeen, what you wear is very important. I asked her, "How is it possible? How did you come to have such beautiful clothes?" She whispered in my ear, "You do this—you do this—you do this . . ." (*Abruptly, to Domenico*) You know that brothel where we met? When I first went there, I thought it was a palace. I only went back to the slum at San Liborio once. My heart thumping in my chest. "They won't speak to me, they'll turn me away, they'll pretend not to know me." But, no. Nobody said a word. Somebody offered me a chair, another touched my hair—I could see it in their eyes—they thought I was better than them! All of them except my mother. When the time came for me to leave, she turned her head the other way. She made no sound but I knew that she was crying. I never went back there again. (*Almost screaming*) I did not kill my sons! A family—a family—I have been thinking of it for twenty-five years. I have brought you up. I have made men of you. I have stolen from him—to give you all you need. All you need.

Michele moves to Filumena

Michele It's all right. It's all right. You did everything you could.

Umberto now moves towards Filumena

Umberto There is so much I would like to say to you, but the words are very difficult to find. I will write them down. I will write you a letter.
Filumena I can't read.
Umberto Then I'd be very happy to read it to you.

Filumena looks towards Riccardo waiting for him too to walk towards her

   Riccardo turns and walks out of the house

Filumena catches at her breath

Umberto He has not understood. I'll call in at his shop tomorrow and explain everything to him.
Michele (*to Filumena*) Come with me. Come home—it's only a small place, but we'll make room for you. It's got a little balcony. (*With a sudden realization*) Hey! Just think! All these

years the kids have asked me about a grandmother! Who is
she? Where is she? Why haven't we got one? All these years
I've had to lie to them and now just think, eh? When we walk
through the door, that will be the first thing I'll shout "Hey,
kids—here's Grandma!" Come on. Come home. Let's go.

Filumena (*decisively*) Yes. I'll come with you.

Michele Let's go then.

Filumena Wait for me by the front door, just two minutes. (*To
Umberto*) You go with him. There's something I have to say
to Don Domenico.

Michele (*delightedly*) Okay, okay! Don't make us wait too long.
(*To Umberto*) Are you coming?

Umberto Yes, yes, I'm coming.

Michele Good-bye, everybody! (*To Umberto, as they go out*)
Do you want to know something? When I got out of bed this
morning, I *knew* something was going to happen.

Umberto and Michele go

Filumena (*indicating the study*) Signor Nocella, would you also
excuse us for a few minutes?

Nocella If you'll excuse *me*—I should go to the office.

Filumena No, please stay. What I have to say to Don Domenico
will not take long—I would rather you were here when I've
finished.

*Nocella shrugs, and goes into the study. Rosalia also makes her-
self scarce*

Filumena puts her bunch of keys on the table

So. I am leaving you, Dummi'. You can tell the solicitor to do
whatever he had to do in order to annul the marriage. I will
put my name to anything he wishes. You are free to do anything you want.

Domenico Why, why? Why did you do this? Filumena, I am a
reasonable man. We could have arranged a settlement between
ourselves. You could have had the money without all this fuss
and argument.

Filumena (*quite calmly*) I will send somebody around tomorrow
—probably Michele—to collect my things.

Domenico You are crazy, that's what you are. You've com-

pletely upset their lives, those three poor boys. What made
you do it?

Filumena (*coldly*) Because one of them is your son.

*Domenico is stunned. He stands for some moments, staring at
Filumena*

Domenico No—no. Shut up, shut up! Don't say any more. . . .

Filumena I could have told you they were all your sons, and you
would have believed it. I would have made you believe it. But
it wouldn't have been true. I could have told you before about
your son, but you would have hated the other two. I wanted
all three to be equal—no difference whatsoever.

Domenico No. No. You're lying!

Filumena No. No. It's true, Dummi'. You wouldn't remember—
you were always going off enjoying yourself—months at a
time. Horses and women. How could you remember one particular night that you spent with me? You know how you
always used to give me a hundred lire note when you left me?
On this particular night you said, "Let's love each other
tonight, Filumena. Let's make love because we really love
each other." And that night I loved you. I really loved you.
But you didn't mean it. And when you switched on the light
again you gave me your usual one hundred lire note. You
know I can't read, but I can write numbers—I wrote the
number of the day and the month on the corner of that note.
Our son was conceived that night, Dummi'. You left—
disappeared again on your usual wanderings. I have never told
you anything because I knew that night meant absolutely
nothing to you.

Domenico No. No. And which one is it?

Filumena Oh, no. I'm not going to tell you that. They must be
equal—all three.

Domenico, frustrated, hesitates

Domenico Filumena, it's not true. It can't be true. If it was true
you would have told me then. You would have used it to tie
me down. A child, a son, would have been a weapon—you
would have used it as a weapon.

Filumena No, no. If I'd told you, you would have made me get
rid of it. That's the way you thought then—and that's the way

you think even today. And because I didn't tell you—that child is alive today. It's *because* I didn't tell you, Dummi', that you have a son.

Domenico Which one?

Filumena No! No. They must all be equal—all three.

Domenico (*angrily*) They are equal—they are whoresons! I don't want to know them! I don't want to know him! I don't want to know you! If I pass you in the street I will not recognize you —get out of my house! If you set foot in this house again, I swear . . .

Filumena Do you remember what I said to you yesterday? Don't swear to anything you couldn't keep, because if you did, you might one day come begging to me? Listen to me, Dummi'. I am going to swear something. If you ever speak one word of what I have told you to any of my sons, I will kill you, Dummi'. I don't say "I will kill you" like you've said it to me for twenty-five years—I say it the way Filumena Marturano says things. I mean it. I will kill you. (*Calling to the study*) I've said what I had to say, Signor Nocella. (*Then, calling to Diana*) And you can come out, too. Don't be afraid—I won't touch you. It's all right. You've won. I'm leaving. The house is yours. (*She calls out again*) Rosalia, Alfredo, Lucia!

Rosalia enters

Filumena embraces her

I want you to put all my things together. I'll send someone around for them tomorrow.

Nocella and Diana enter from the study. Alfredo also appears from the kitchen

Take care of yourselves. (*To Rosalia*) Will you get me my coat? Signor Nocella—Don Domenico will tell you what you have to do.

Lucia enters. Rosalia fetches a coat from the bedroom

Now, Domenico. Once again, in front of all these people, I'll tell you what I said to you earlier is strictly between the two of us. (*She takes her locket from round her neck and opens it. She takes out and unfolds a tightly wrapped one hundred lire note*) I've kept this a long time! There is something written on one corner that I still need. (*She tears off a corner of the note and hands the rest of it to Domenico*) Here. Take it. It belongs to you. It can buy many things. It can't buy a son.

Filumena goes out, as—

the CURTAIN *falls*

ACT III

Ten months later, early evening

There are flowers everywhere, some in bouquets, some arranged in elegant baskets with greetings cards from their senders. The flowers should be in delicate colours—not red or white. There is a general atmosphere of celebration

Rosalia enters from the outer door. She is dressed in her Sunday best. At the same time, Domenico enters from the study. He has changed. He is a quieter, less bombastic man than the one we knew before. His hair is a shade whiter

Domenico Have you been out?

Rosalia Yes.

Domenico Where to?

Rosalia On a secret assignment for Donna Filumena. I have sworn not to breathe a word to a living soul.

Domenico Not even to me?

Rosalia Least of all to you. If you were the last person alive on earth you would have to find someone else to tell you. It's just between her and me. You're not jealous, are you? At your age, too!

Domenico What do you mean—jealous? What has my age got to do with it?

Rosalia Don't worry. It was only a joke. Ask me again where I have been.

Domenico Where have you been?

Rosalia To a certain street in San Liborio. Now ask me what for.

Domenico What for?

Rosalia That is what I am not allowed to tell you. My lips are sealed.

Domenico All right then, keep it to yourself. I don't want to know.

Rosalia No, I'm going to tell you, because I think you ought to know. She gave me one thousand lire early this morning, and fifty candles. She asked me to take them to the shrine of the Madonna of the Roses in a street of San Liborio. There's an old woman—who takes care of the shrine. The one thousand lire are for flowers and the lamp, but the fifty candles are all going to be lit at six o'clock this evening, on the dot. Do you know why she chose six o'clock?

Domenico Yes, yes, I do.

Rosalia No, you don't. Because the marriage is taking place at six o'clock. While you are here, getting married, the candles will be lit up in front of the Madonna of the Roses at exactly the same time.

Domenico That's good. I like the idea.

Rosalie But the woman's very old. I hope it works. Donna Filumena is a saint. You know that you're marrying a saint? You should be very proud. It isn't everyone that gets to marry a saint, you know.

Domenico I'm a lucky man. I know, I know.

Rosalia She's also very beautiful. She looks younger every day. She's too good for you. I used to tell her, "Don Domenico will come round running after you, asking for you back again," I'd say. "Don't worry," I told her, "he only had the marriage annulled because he's a proud man and a stubborn old fool."

Domenico Donna Rosalia, go and help Filumena.

Rosalia I'm going, I'm going. But it's you who should be giving thanks to the Madonna today, not her. And me. Yes, I don't know what would have become of me if it had not been for Donna Filumena. She brought me into her house when I had no-one. I shall stay here until my dying day.

Domenico That's entirely up to you.

Rosalia I'm all prepared for that day.

Domenico What day?

Rosalia The big day. I've everything ready in a drawer in my room. A long white dress, trimmed with lace. White stockings. A white cap. It's all there. Donna Filumena knows where I keep it. Nobody is going to lay a finger on me—only her. She has promised me that. In any case, there is nobody but her. I used to pray perhaps one of my own sons might turn up again one day ... Don Domenico, excuse me please, I'm rather busy.

Rosalia goes out to the bedroom

Domenico wanders about the room, looking at the flowers, examining the cards

Domenico (*speaking a thought out loud*) So be it. So be it.

We hear the voices of the Three Sons before they enter

Michele (*off*) Six o'clock. The wedding takes place at six o'clock.

Riccardo (*off*) I don't care what time the wedding's fixed for, we were supposed to meet downstairs at five.

Umberto (*off*) I *was* here at five.

Michele, Riccardo and Umberto enter, continuing the conversation

Michele I would have been here at five, too—but I didn't know what time it was.

Riccardo If you were going to be late, you should have let us know.

Michele I wasn't late. In Naples, if you have an appointment for five o'clock—you don't get there at five o'clock—five o'clock means five-thirty or a quarter to six.

Riccardo Or the day after, or next month . . .

Michele If my watch hadn't been broken, I'd have been here before either of you.

Riccardo You should have it mended.

Michele It's been mended. That's why it does not work. The kids mended it. There was nothing wrong with it before. Now that it's been mended it won't go.

Umberto What do you mean—it's been mended?

Umberto is the first to see Domenico. He greets him respectfully

Umberto Good evening, Don Domenico. I didn't see you standing there.

Domenico Good evening, Umberto.

Riccardo (*also with respect*) Good evening, Don Domenico.

Domenico Good evening, Riccardo.

Michele (*again with respect*) Don Domenico.

Domenico Michele.

All three of them stand in front of Domenico. There is an awkward silence

What? You've stopped talking. As soon as you see me, you
stop talking. Please go on with what you were saying.
Umberto We were just discussing generalities . . .
Riccardo Nothing important . . .
Michele And we came to the end of what we had to say.
Domenico (*fetching a decanter of sherry and glasses on a tray, from
the sideboard*) At exactly the same moment you set eyes on me.
Please, let's sit down.

They all sit. Domenico pours drinks

The wedding's not until six o'clock, so we've lots of time before
the priest arrives. We haven't invited any other guests—so
there'll be just us, eh? That's how Filumena wanted it. And
she's right. After twenty-five years of wrong living we are
going to put things straight. It's called a reparation marriage.
Not before time—eh? But here—in private. Could you see us
going into a church? It's better the priest comes here. *Saluté*.
Michele ⎫
Umberto ⎬ *Saluté*, Don Domenico. (*Speaking together*)
Riccardo ⎭

They all drink

Domenico Listen. There is one thing I'd like to say—I've mentioned it before—I'd rather you didn't keep calling me Don
Domenico.
Umberto Yes, I remember you saying so.
Riccardo Several times.
Michele That's right.
Umberto But you didn't tell us, Don Domenico—how would you
like us to address you?
Domenico Well, I thought you might have understood the situation and—er—come up with something. Your mother and I
we're getting married tonight and—well—listen, there's another thing I want to tell you. I've seen my lawyer. He's fixed
things up. Tomorrow you'll have my name—Soriano.

*Umberto, Michele and Riccardo exchange embarrassed glances,
each hoping another will speak first. Finally, Umberto clears his
throat*

Umberto I'd like to speak on behalf of all three of us, if that's all

right by you, sir. We have discussed the situation and . . .
You see, it's not as if we were children any more. We're three
grown men. We really appreciate the fact that you want to give
us your name—even though it may cause us a few problems.

Domenico What problems?

Umberto Legally it's very easy to take on someone else's name
overnight, but it will be a little difficult to adjust to coping with
a new name, a family . . .

Riccardo Parents, a mother, stepfather . . .

Michele You see, Don Domenico, there are some things that can
only come from the heart.

Domenico Yes. Yes. I understand this. And what you are saying,
all of you, you cannot find it in your hearts to call me "father"
or "papa" or . . . (*He tails off*)

Umberto Don Domenico, I respect you. That is why I cannot lie
to you. You don't deserve that. But for the time being—
really—no.

Domenico And you?

Riccardo Well—I—I'm sorry, no.

Domenico How about you, Michele?

Michele I can't, Don Domenico. I'd like to, but I can't.

Domenico Okay. I understand this. With time . . . One gets
accustomed to it. I see—yes . . . Anyway, I'm happy to be
here with you. And do you know why I'm happy? Although I
don't know you very well yet—I feel you are good boys. You're
honest boys, I like that. You all work, in one field or another,
but you all work hard. Do you know something? I'm really
proud of you. (*To Umberto*) You've qualified as an accountant,
not only that but you also write articles.

Umberto A few little stories, that's all.

Domenico But you get them published. People read them. People
pay for them. Who knows, in a few years' time, perhaps we'll
have a best-selling author in the family?

Umberto I can't expect that much.

Domenico You must expect that much, Umberto. That's how
you'll succeed. Push yourself. Drive yourself. I only wish I had
gone on with it. I was a writer myself at your age.

Umberto You were a writer?

Domenico Oh yes. Nothing much—just a few poems. You know
how it is when you're in love with a girl. You write poems.

Umberto I'd very much like to read some of them.

Domenico No, they're gone now. I stopped a long time ago. I didn't have the dedication. Umberto—if that's inside you from the start you'll do it, believe me.

Umberto I don't think I have got that *kind* of dedication. To be a writer.

Domenico Tell me about it.

Umberto Sometimes I feel that isn't me at all. I've tried so many things. Once I had a drawing lesson. Now I've taken up the violin. Sometimes I tell myself I've made a mistake—I think I should be doing something quite different.

Domenico (*keenly interested*) What do you think that you would like to do with your life?

Umberto When you're young, you want to do everything.

Domenico I know.

Riccardo Take me. I never intended to go into the retail clothing business. When I was at school I didn't see myself measuring men for shirts. Shall I tell you how it happened? I was crazy about a girl who worked a sewing-machine. So I got myself a job in the same factory as her. I became a shirt-maker because I was having that girl.

Domenico Oh? You've had a lot of girls, eh?

Riccardo (*with a modest shrug*) I do all right. I can't complain.

Sensing a clue to the identity of his son, Domenico studies Riccardo closely, looking for a recognizable gesture or mannerism

Domenico You never felt like settling down?

Riccardo You know the way it is with me. I never seem to find the right type. I meet a girl—I like her—I say, "This is it! That's the girl!" And immediately I decide to marry her. But then I meet another one, and I think I like her much more.

Domenico You can't make up your mind?

Riccardo I don't know what it is. I can't understand it. It seems to me that there is always a woman I like better than the one I've just met.

Domenico Extraordinary.

Riccardo Well, let's say I've never yet found the right one.

Umberto You'd go with anything, Riccardo.

Domenico (*to Umberto*) You're not at all like your brother as far as women are concerned, are you?

Umberto Hold on—I like girls.

Domenico You like girls, too?

Umberto Oh yes, and how. The problem is, with girls today you have to be very careful. You meet a lot of very attractive women, and the choice is very difficult. What can you do? The only thing to do is to change one after the other until you find the right one.

Riccardo That's what I said.

Umberto Yes, but with a little more discrimination, Riccardo.

Domenico (*disappointedly*) So you too like to change girls one after the other?

Umberto Yes. Exactly. Why settle for anything until you have found the right one?

Domenico (*to Michele*) What about you? Do you like women as much as your brothers?

Michele Oh, Mother of God, I'm afraid I met the right one when I was nineteen. I met my wife and—good-bye for ever. We'd only been married four months when she dropped the first one. A year later, along came number two. We've got number four now running round the house. I don't mind. I happen to like kids.

Domenico You're a happily married man. You don't look at other women.

Michele Of course I look at other women. I look at them all the time. With the mouths I have to feed, looking is all I can afford. Besides, you should see my wife. She's not a woman, she's an armoured tank. If she caught me at it, she'd crush me into the ground.

Domenico (*disgruntled*) But given the money and the opportunity, and you'd be worse than either of those. (*He pauses, and tries another subject*) When I was young I was a very good singer. We used to go to this open-air restaurant. One guy would bring along his mandolin, another one had a guitar. A warm night, dinner under the stars, a dozen bottles of wine, and we would open up our hearts and our voices . . . (*He sings a snatch of a song then stops*) Which one of you's the singer?

Umberto Not me.

Riccardo Me neither.

Michele (*over-modestly*) I do a little singing, now and then.

Domenico You do, Michele?

Michele Nearly all the time. If I work, I sing. It's in my nature.
If I have a spanner in my hand, I have a song in my mouth.

Domenico Let me hear something?

Michele Do you have a spanner?

Umberto ⎫
Riccardo ⎬ Sing, sing (*Speaking together*)

Michele I don't sing for other people—I only sing for my own
amusement.

Domenico Sing for me. It's my wedding day. When a man gets
married he's entitled to a song.

Michele Well—all right. What would you like?

Domenico Anything. You choose. Whatever you like.

*Michele strikes a pose and starts to sing but he is hopelessly out of
tune*

Michele (*singing*)

> On a Sunday in September
> There's a girl that I remember
> Took a walk beside a mountain
> To a convent with a fountain
> Made a vow and broke my heart
> I can't believe it—it can't be true.

Riccardo (*interrupting*) You don't call that singing, do you?

Michele If you can do any better, you sing it.

Umberto I could do better than that.

Riccardo Of course. You play the violin—you sing.

Umberto So I play the violin. It doesn't mean I can sing.

Domenico Riccardo, you try.

Riccardo No, no—I don't sing. Well, occasionally—I sing.

*Riccardo starts to sing. He is just as bad as Michele. Umberto
joins in. He is also badly out of tune. And now Michele joins in. As
soloists they are bad enough, but as a trio they are worse*

(*Singing*)

> On a Sunday in September
> There's a girl that I remember
> Took a walk beside a mountain

Umberto ⎫ To a convent with a fountain   ⎫ (*Singing*
Riccardo ⎰ Made a vow and broke my heart   ⎰ together*)

Umberto ⎤	I can't believe it—it can't be true
Riccardo ⎬	Beside a convent fountain
Michele ⎦	Close to Napoli

⎫ (*Singing*
⎬ *together*)
⎭

Domenico Stop! Stop!

The singers tail off

Domenico It isn't possible—I don't believe it. Three Neapolitans, and not one of them can hit a note!

Filumena enters from the bedroom. She is wearing a beautiful dress. Her hair is piled high in the Neapolitan manner. She is wearing ear rings and two strings of pearls. She looks younger. She is accompanied by her dressmaker, Teresina. Rosalia follows them. Lucia enters from the kitchen

Filumena It is *not* all right, Teresina. It is quite wrong. (*Holding out her arms*) Look! This sleeve is at least four centimetres shorter than this one.

Teresina is one of those Neapolitan dressmakers who are immune to criticism from their clients. Her imperturbability makes her all the more aggravating

Teresina No, no—it's all in your mind, Donna Filumena. They are both the same. It's the way you're standing. The dress is fine—don't forget, you're right arm is a little longer than your left one. It always has been—I should know your measurements, I've been making dresses for you all these years.

Filumena Don't try to insult my intelligence, Teresina. My arms are both the same length—I have had them longer than I've had you for a dressmaker. I should know! It's the dress. The right sleeve is shorter than the left.

Teresina All right, all right. If you say so. The left sleeve is longer than the right.

Filumena It isn't just the sleeves, Teresina, it's too tight in the waist. Do you know why it's too tight in the waist? Because whenever I buy a piece of cloth that is big enough to make a dress for me—you cut off a metre and a half to make a frock for your little girl.

Teresina What! I have never stolen any material from you for a frock for little Carla.

Filumena Don't argue with me, Teresina! I have seen it happen, with these eyes. I walk down the street in a dress you have made and seen your Carla playing in the gutter in a dress identical to mine.

Teresina Yes, yes, Donna Filumena. If any material is left over at the end, I take it—yes—but I don't steal it first.

Filumena gives her a reproving look. Teresina has completed her temporary alteration to the sleeve, and now steps back for general approbation of her work

Rosalia (*almost overcome with admiration*) Oh, it's wonderful! It's beautiful! Donna Filumena, you're a young bride.

Filumena (*to Teresina, ignoring Rosalia*) In future, if there is any material left over, you bring it back to me.

Teresina All right, all right. If it's like the last time, I'll bring it back to you and then you can throw it away. It's too small for anything else . . .

Domenico who has been watching all of this with his mind elsewhere, now interrupts

Domenico Filumena, can I talk to you?

Filumena takes a few steps towards Domenico, hobbling in her new shoes

Filumena These shoes, these shoes!
Domenico Take them off if they're hurting you.
Filumena And get married in bare feet?
Domenico Wear an old pair. We're not going anywhere.

Filumena "tut-tuts" irritatedly at the suggestion

Filumena What do you want to talk to me about?
Domenico (*to the Three Sons*) Please, will you excuse us? Wait in the study? Get yourselves a drink.
Michele Come on, you two.
Riccardo (*to Michele, as they go*) The singing plumber—you missed your way—you should be appearing at the Opera House.
Michele Do you think so?
Umberto Yes. Changing the washers on the taps in the dressing-rooms.

Laughing, Umberto, Michele and Riccardo go into the study. Lucia exits to the kitchen

Domenico Teresina, if you wouldn't mind . . .

Teresina I'm going, Don Domenico. I'm on my way right now. Congratulations—I hope you'll both be very happy and enjoy many years of married life in each other's company. (*To Rosalia, as she goes out*) I don't like to tell her, but it's not that her left arm is shorter than the other; it's her right shoulder that droops.

Teresina goes out by the outer door. Rosalia follows her

Domenico replaces the sherry tray on the sideboard, then stands for a moment admiring Filumena

Domenico You look wonderful. Like a young girl. If only I could think straight, I would tell you that you would turn any man's head.

Filumena senses the subject that he is about to raise—and tries to evade it

Filumena My head's been in a whirl all day. So many things to think about—I hope I haven't forgotten anything.

Domenico Filumena, there is something on my mind.

Filumena If I *have* forgotten something, we must hope that Lucia puts it right. We can't rely on Rosalia or Alfredo, they're getting very old . . .

Domenico You know what I mean, Filume'. Don't change the subject. I haven't been able to think clearly for months. And you are the only one who can give me peace of mind.

Filumena Me?

Domenico Yes. Haven't I done everything for you that you wanted me to do? After the marriage had been annulled I called round to see you not once, but many times. Every time I got the same answer. That you were not in. Every time I knew that you were there—and every time I went away and came back again in a day or two.

Filumena So?

Domenico So when you finally agreed to see me, I asked you to marry me.

Filumena And tonight that marriage is taking place.

Domenico Have I made you happy, Filumena? I want you to be happy.

Filumena Yes—yes, of course . . .

Domenico But you have to make me happy too. Sit down, please. Listen to what I have to say.

Filumena sits down

Domenico If you only knew how many times these past months I've tried to talk to you, but I just couldn't bring myself to do so. All my life I've been a proud man—above all else, I think, I have had this man's pride. With all my strength, I have tried to overcome that pride. But there are some things that will not easily come out of my mouth. I know that this is a subject that you would much rather I did not raise now, but we are getting married, you and I. In only a few more moments we shall kneel together before God, Filumi'. We are not taking these marriage vows like a young couple who believe that love is something which they share from the warmth of each other in the dark of the night. We are not young people, Filumena. I am fifty-two years old and you are forty-eight. We are old enough, surely, to realize what we are doing, we understand what getting married means. It's a serious business. You know why you are marrying me—but I don't know why I am marrying you. The only reason I can think of is that I am marrying you because you have told me that one of those three boys is my son.

Filumena Only for that?

Domenico No. Not only for that. I love you, Filumena. I am marrying you because I believe that we need each other. I am marrying you because I believe it is right. (*Striking his chest*) I feel it in here. It's only because I am so close to you, that I can begin to tell you these things. (*Deeply serious*) Filumena, at night I don't sleep—I have hardly slept at all since that night ten months ago when you said what you said and walked out of this house. I don't sleep, I don't eat, I don't go out—it's as if I was dead, Filumi'. You don't know what is going on inside me. It is as if I can't breathe. I go like this—(*he takes a deep breath*)—and the breath sticks here. (*He points to his throat*) You mustn't make me go on like this. You have a heart. You are a woman who knows life and can understand how much this means to me. Show me you love me, Filumena.

You cannot make me live like this. Do you remember when you told me not to make that vow? If I swore false, you said, I would one day come begging at your feet. Look, Filumena, I am begging now, kissing your hands. Tell me—tell me which one is my flesh, my blood, which one of those three boys is my son. It is for your sake as well as mine. For if you do not tell me, for the rest of my life there will be a suspicion in my heart that I was blackmailed into marriage. Please tell me now, Filumena. I swear that I'll still marry you.

Filumena gives him a long, hard look

Filumena Very well. Supposing I say to you, "That one is your son". What will you do? You'll put your arms around him, kiss him, plan his future, find ways of giving him money that you wouldn't give to the other two.

Domenico Why not?

Filumena Yes, why not? Then help him—he needs it.

Domenico Michele. The plumber.

Filumena Rosalia says he's a sanitary engineer.

Domenico A plumber? So? It's a good trade to have. He's a good boy. Strong, like me. He's a worker. If he hadn't married when he was just a boy he'd have done better for himself in business. But it's not too late now for him to expand. We can find some larger premises, take on some extra staff. He could control things from the office . . . (*He glances suspiciously at Filumena*) Wait a moment. The plumber. The family man. The one who needs the money most? What a coincidence!

Filumena (*pretending disappointment*) What would any mother do? Try to help the one who needs it most. All right, you're too clever for me. It isn't Michele.

Domenico It's Riccardo.

Filumena No, it isn't.

Domenico It's Umberto.

Filumena No, it isn't.

Domenico Are you going to torture me for the rest of my life?

Filumena is moved by Domenico's depth of feeling. She tries to find words that will make him understand the real situation

Filumena Listen to me, Dummi', listen carefully—and then we shall never bring up this subject again. I have always loved you with all my heart and with all my strength. To me, you have always been a god. I would never have believed it possible, but today I love you more than I have ever done before. What have you done, Dummi'? It's not me that tortures you, you are bringing this torture upon yourself. God gave you everything that any man could ask for. Your health, your strength, he made you handsome—he even led you to me, because he knew that I would give my life for you, if that was what you wanted. I need not have told you about the children. I could have gone on, taking your money, giving it to them and never saying a word. Please. Never ask me again which one is yours. I must not tell you. And you must have the strength to never ask me. Because if, in a moment of weakness, I told you, it would ruin all our lives. Didn't you see, yourself? When I said Michele was your son, your mind went straight to money. Buy him a bigger place. Help him to expand.

Domenico Why not?

Filumena Because you say to yourself, quite naturally "Why can't I help? Why can't I tell him?—I'm his father." And what would happen then to the other two? What would they think of him? What would he think of them? They are three brothers and you would set them at each other's throats. They are three grown men—they are not children. Don't think of yourself, Dummi'. Don't think of me. Think of them. We missed the beautiful days of loving them as children. Children are those wonderful little things that you pick up in your arms when they are not well, and they cannot tell you what they feel. We'll never pick them up, hold them and kiss and cuddle them as we should have held them and kissed them. Or when they come running to you with their arms open—"Mama, Papa!" Coming home from school with cold hands and red noses "I was good in class today, Papa, give me a present!" No, we shall never know those moments. They are three grown men. Either they are all equal or they are enemies. (*She pauses*) There is still time, Domenico. Either that or let us finish, you and I. It's not too late. We can still go our separate ways.

The organ strikes up in the study

Rosalia enters. Umberto, Michele and Riccardo also enter, from the study

Rosalia He's here—the priest has just arrived!
Michele Mother—

Domenico rises. He has arrived at a decision

Domenico Let us finish now and go our separate ways. (*To the Three Sons*) I have something to say to you. I have always been proud to call myself an honest man and I cannot live a lie. Listen to me, please.

Umberto
Michele }Yes, Father? }(*Speaking together*)
Riccardo

Domenico (*with a glance at Filumena, making up his mind*) Thank you. You have made me very happy. (*Suddenly cheerful*) Very well, then—when a man and woman marry, it is the duty of the bride's father to lead her to the altar. Today, there are no parents present—only sons. Two of you will take your mother up the aisle, the other will escort the bridegroom.

Filumena (*remembering something*) What time is it?

Riccardo Five minutes to six.

Filumena Five to six! Rosalia . . .?

Rosalia Don't worry. Everything is taken care of. It's all going to happen just as you have arranged.

Filumena (*taking the arms of Michele and Riccardo*) I'm ready.

Filumena, Michele and Riccardo go into the study. Domenico and Umberto follow

The organ strikes up the "Wedding March". Rosalia begins to cry

Alfredo and Lucia enter and, with Rosalia, follow the others into the study

The Lights dim to total darkness. Time has passed. A beam of moonlight strikes the room from the terrace. And then the Lights fade up in the dining-room

Filumena enters from the study carrying a spray of wedding flowers, accompanied by Umberto, Michele and Rosalia. Lucia enters from the kitchen with a tray of glasses

Filumena I am so tired.

Michele Come and sit down. It's time we were going.

Filumena sits

Rosalia Congratulations—congratulations, many, many congratulations. Especially you, my daughter—all these years,
you've been like a daughter to me! And now you are Signora
Soriano!

*Riccardo and Domenico enter from the study. Domenico has a
bottle of expensive wine, the cork smothered in wax*

Riccardo Well—no last-minute problems, everything went like
clockwork.

Filumena Rosalia, bring me a glass of water, please.

Rosalia (*enthusiastically*) Right away, Signora Soriano! Immediately, Signora Soriano!

Domenico (*pouring drinks*) Who wants water?

Rosalia Your wife. It's for the mistress of the house.

Domenico Would you tell my wife from her husband that nobody
drinks water on his wedding night. And Alfredo, too. Where
is he, Alfredo Amoroso, the well-known sportsman, the famous
jockey?

Rosalia (*calling towards the kitchen*) Alfri', Alfri', come and drink
a glass of wine with your master! Luci', you as well!

Alfredo enters

Alfredo I am here!

Domenico looks at Alfredo with nostalgic affection

Domenico Remember, Alfri'? When our horses thundered down
the course? What a thrill it gave us?

Alfredo Mother of God!

Domenico Well, now the race is over. They've passed the post.
The jockey's have weighed in, old friend. Yes, the race is finished.
(*He gestures at the three sons*) Now it's their turn to saddle up.
We'd make fools of ourselves, Alfredo, if we attempted to ride
with them.

Alfredo We would . . . We would . . .

Domenico Filumena, you first. Everyone take a glass.

Filumena rises. They all drink

A child is a child. A son is a son. They come from God. When there is more than one child in a family, it's not unusual for the father to have a favourite. For any reason. Perhaps he likes this one the most because he's the strongest, perhaps he takes to the one that is the ugliest, or the weakest of the bunch, perhaps he chooses one that is a little crazier than all the others. The rest of the family doesn't mind. "That one is Father's boy," they say. It's the old man's privilege. This could never happen to us, because our family got together too late. And that's good, because this privilege I have of being allowed to love one particular son will be shared between all three. (*He drinks*) *Saluté*. To our family.

Filumena says nothing. She holds her spray of wedding flowers and smells them occasionally

Michele Sorry, I must go now. I've left the wife and children at home.

Domenico (*to the sons*) Tomorrow you are all expected for dinner.

Michele Can I bring my wife?

Domenico Of course—and the children.

Riccardo I'm afraid I can't tomorrow, Father. I have a very important business engagement.

Domenico Business! Bring her, too.

Riccardo Can I? Thanks, Father. (*He goes to Filumena*) We're going to leave you now. It's late, and Mother's tired, she needs her rest. Be happy, Mother. (*He kisses her*) Congratulations—and we'll look forward to seeing you tomorrow.

Umberto (*also kissing Filumena*) Good-night, take care of yourself.

Michele (*doing the same*) Good-night, Mama—see you tomorrow.

Umberto Good-night, Father.

Michele Until tomorrow, Father.

Riccardo Good-night, Papa.

Lucia, Alfredo and Rosalia exit to the kitchen. Umberto, Michele and Riccardo exit by the outer door

Domenico Until tomorrow. Don't be late, Michele.

Domenico watches the boys go, deep in thought. He goes to the table and pours himself another drink. Filumena sits in the armchair and takes off her shoes

Filumena Mother of God, I am so tired, Dummi'. I feel it all
   now—altogether.
Domenico It's been hard for you. All the emotion and the
   worries of the last few days. You can relax now. You'll sleep
   well tonight. I'll finish this drink and we'll go to bed. (*He goes
   towards the terrace*) It's been a beautiful day. It's a beautiful
   evening, too.

*Something catches at Filumena's throat making her give a slight
moan, and then she lets out a deep sigh. She looks into emptiness
and the tears stream down her face. Domenico is concerned and
crosses towards her*

Domenico Filumi', what's the matter? What is it?
Filumena I'm crying, Dummi'—I'm crying. I'm crying.

CURTAIN

FURNITURE AND PROPERTY LIST

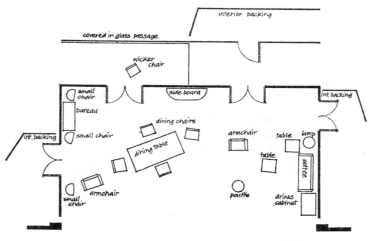

ACT I

On stage: Ornate sideboard. *On it:* silver cups and trophies, clock, various china and other ornaments

Bureau

Dining-table. *On it:* lace cloth covering half, crockery, glass and cutlery for meal for two, jug of water, bowl of red roses

Drinks cabinet. *In it:* various bottles and decanters, glasses

2 occasional tables

2 armchairs

Settee

Pouffe

4 dining-chairs

3 small chairs

Wicker chair

On walls: old family photographs, painting, tapestry

Off stage: Tray with covered dishes containing spring chickens and elaborate sweet, box with bottles of wine **(Waiters)**

Basket with several pharmaceutical parcels and nurse's overall **(Diana)**

Domenico's jacket **(Alfredo)**

ACT II

Strike: Everything from table
Overall and parcels

Set: Some chairs on table, other furniture cleared for **Lucia** to
wash floor
Cloth and bucket of water on floor

Off stage: Cup of coffee **(Lucia)**
Briefcase with papers and law book **(Nocella)**
Plumber's bag of tools **(Michele)**
Filumena's coat **(Rosalia)**

Personal: **Umberto:** notebook, pencil
Riccardo: wristwatch
Michele: half-smoked cigarette
Filumena: bunch of keys, locket containing 100-lire note

ACT III

Strike: Coffee cup
Bunch of keys
Note

Set: Baskets and vases of flowers with greetings cards, on table
and other furniture
Fancy cloth on table

Off stage: Opened bottle of wine **(Domenico)**
Tray of glasses **(Lucia)**
Dressmaking materials **(Teresina)**
Spray of wedding flowers, fan **(Filumena)**

LIGHTING PLOT

Property fittings required: ornate pendant, standard lamp
Interior. A dining-room. The same scene throughout

ACT I	Late afternoon	
To open:	General effect of fading afternoon sunlight	
Cue 1	**Diana** exits *Slow fade to dusk*	(Page 16)
Cue 2	**Domenico** switches on lights *Snap on pendant and standard lamp*	(Page 18)

ACT II   Morning

To open: General effect of bright sunny day

No cues

ACT III   Evening

To open: General effect of early evening daylight

Cue 3	After **Teresina**'s exit *Slow fade to dusk*	(Page 57)
Cue 4	On general exit for wedding *Fade to Black-out: bring up beam of moonlight* *across stage: snap on full interior lighting, pendant* *and standard lamp, after brief pause*	(Page 57)

EFFECTS PLOT

ACT I

Cue 1	**Filumena:** "This house is mine." *Doorbell rings*	(Page 13)

ACT II

Cue 2	**Diana:** ". . . he went into it very fully . . ." *Doorbell rings*	(Page 29)
Cue 3	**Lucia** moves to bedroom *Doorbell rings*	(Page 30)
Cue 4	**Riccardo:** "When are you coming?" *Doorbell rings*	(Page 31)

ACT III

Cue 5	**Filumena:** ". . . go our separate ways." *Organ music from study*	(Page 60)
Cue 6	**Filumena:** "I'm ready." *Organ strikes up Wedding March*	(Page 61)

MADE AND PRINTED IN GREAT BRITAIN BY
LATIMER TREND & COMPANY LTD PLYMOUTH
MADE IN ENGLAND